Introduction

When we decided that a cookery book was a good, on going, way of raising money for F-IVF, Ruari and I had no idea of what it would involve, neither of us having had any dealings with the world of printing and publishing. We had thought initially that I would write to not only the most well known names in cooking, but also other highly recommended chefs and cooks from hotels and restaurants all over the U.K.

In my naivete I thought, as each wave of letters was posted, that I would be inundated with replies. Wrong of course. Eventually, an excellent twenty three percent of all those letters bore fruit, and what a harvest. Upwards of 200 recipes. Some simple, everyday, others grandiose. Some friendly, informative, chatty and those straight from the professional kitchen file. From Fillet of Goosnargh Chicken studded with Truffle, for one, to Meat Sauce - Traditional Bolognese which requires 60 lbs. of mince. Meringues with Passion Fruit and Oranges to Salade Aphrodite. A Victorian Breakfast to Afternoon Tea.

My thanks to all those very busy people who sent not only their work but their good wishes too, for the success of the book. A special thank you to Derek Cooper for the Foreword and to Mike Goring, a good friend, who spent so much time producing the illustrations which enhance these pages.

I have enjoyed the time spent collecting these recipes together and tasting the end results in many cases (thanks to Ruari's expertise in the kitchen). We have even met some of the people who sent us entries and hope to meet more on our travels in the future.

Mostly, thanks to you who have bought this book and made all the enjoyment and time taken worthwhile - and in the words of Albert Roux " 'APPY COOKING "!

Sue Cilliers

Foreword

by

Derek Cooper

You might, just by walking round the supermarkets, be tempted to believe that everyone in Britain has given up cooking for good. It has almost happened in New York where everybody either eats out or out of the freezer. Once a month a few kindred friends will be gathered in to watch the host or hostess demonstrate their skills. The atmosphere at such cook-ins is almost like attending the ritual reconstruction of a long-lost tribal art. Shrill cries of wonder fill the kitchen as Hal does his Red Snapper Cajun-style with mung beans and wabadabe noodles as revealed in last month's Gourmet. And when Charlene whips up her tortilla toasties in a pecan tulip and opens a bottle of boutique Blance Fumé, joy knows no bounds.

If we don't get back into the kitchen immediately I see it happening here. Already in the last year I have been out to dinner twice to eat a menu trollied in from Marks and Spencer. Nothing wrong with dear old M&S, I've worn their socks for years but I'd rather they didn't cater for dinner parties.

When I go out I like to find someone has actually bought raw materials – vegetables, fruit, meat, fish – and done well by them. I don't want to be astonished with gastronomic pyrotechnics but just fed good food in season.

The art of cooking is as important as painting, literature, music or any other. It is far too central a part of family life to leave it to some factory to do it for you all the time. A family that eats together may not stay together but at least they can sit round a table and enjoy fresh food straight from the stove with perhaps the bonus of a little food talk.

I like to know how my food has been prepared; how it comes to taste so good and what went into it. I made an embarrassing gaffe at one of these M&S dinner parties by asking what was in the sauce – something indefinable I couldn't identify. Was it cumin perhaps? Half way through asking the question I suddenly realised that the only way my hostess could provide the answer was by going out to the garbage can and looking at the ingredients list on the box. It quite ruined the evening.

This book contains scores of excellent ways of not ruining lunch or dinner. Su Gillies is to be congratulated on winkling these fine recipes from so many distinguished cooks – they celebrate the joy of fresh food and the great pleasure that can be achieved from pleasing others.

So to the kitchen and bon appetit!

Derek Cooper

Writer and broadcaster. Presenter of Radio 4's The Food Programme

FROM HIGHLANDS TO ISLANDS -

A COOK'S TOUR

RECIPES FROM AROUND BRITAIN

compiled by Su Gillies

foreword by Derek Cooper

illustrations by Mike Goring

First published in 1990

Published in aid of The Friends of In Vitro Fertilisation
at John Radcliffe Hospital, Oxford
Proceeds to F-IVF

Published by Su Gillies
5 The Links, Welwyn Garden City,
Hertfordshire, AL8 7DS

ISBN 0-9516955-0-9

Printed by Adept Press, 273 Abbeydale Road, Wembley, Middlesex HA0 1PZ. Tel: 081-998 2247
A commercial litho printing company staffed mainly by deaf people run as a co-operative.

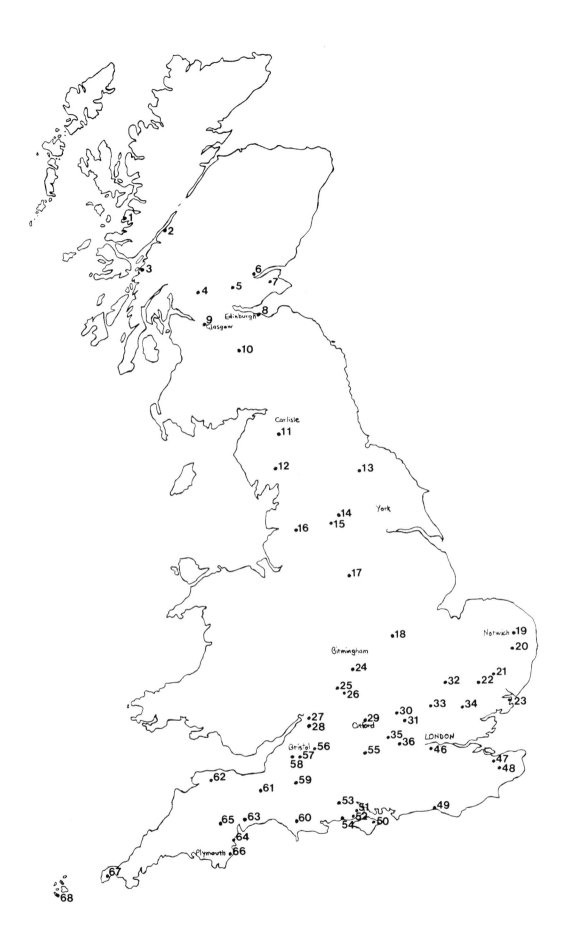

1
•2
•3
6•
5• •7
4•
•8
9• Edinburgh•
Glasgow
•10

Carlisle
•11

•12 •13

•14 York
•15
•16

•17

•18 Norwich •19
•20
Birmingham
•24 •32 21•
22•
•25 •33 •34 23
•26 •30 •31
29• •35
Oxford •36 LONDON
27• 55• •46 •47
28• •48
Bristol •56
•57 •49
58
•62 •59 53• 51
61• 52•
•60 54• •50
65• •63
•64
Plymouth •66
•67
68

1. Arisaig House, Arisaig,
2. Inverlochy Castle, Fort William,
3. Isle of Eriska, Oban
4. Braeval Old Mill, Aberfoyle
5. The Gleneagles Hotel, Auchterarder
6. The Murrayshall, Scone
7. Ostler Close Restaurant, Cupar
8. Skippers Bistro, Leith
9. Rogano Seafood Bar, Glasgow
10. Shieldhill, Biggar
11. Sharrow Bay Hotel, Lake Ullswater
12. Miller Howe Hotel, Windermere
13. Kirkby Fleetham Hall, Northallerton
14. Pool Court Restaurant, Pool-in-Wharfedale
15. The Belvedere Hotel, Bradford
16. Northcote Manor, Langho
17. Cavendish Hotel, Baslow
18. Hambleton Hall. Hambleton
19. Adlards Restaurant, Norwich
20. a) The Fox and Goose, Fressingfield, Diss
    b) Salisbury House Restaurant, Diss
21. Delia Smith
22. The Great House, Lavenham
23. The Pier at Harwich, Harwich
24. Mallory Court, Leamington Spa
25. The Lygon Arms, Broadway
26. The Marsh Goose, Moreton-in-Marsh
27. Oakes Restaurant, Stroud
28. Calcot Manor, Tetbury
29. Browns Restaurant, Oxford
30. The Bell Inn, Aston Clinton
31. The Kings Arms, Old Amersham
32. The Pink Geranium, Melbourn
33. Heath Lodge Hotel, Welwyn
34. Rumbles Cottage Restaurant, Felsted
35. The Stonor Arms, Henley-on-Thames
36. Cliveden, Taplow
37. Le Gavroche, London
38. La Tante Claire, London
39. Food For Thought, London
40. The Ritz, London
41. Langans Brasserie, London
42. La Bastide, London
43. Leith's, London
44. Inigo jones, London
45. Josceline Dimbleby
46. Les Alouettes, Claygate
47. Read's, Faversham
48. Micheal Barry
49. Le Grandgousier, Brighton
50. Seaview Hotel, Seaview
51. The Montagu Arms, Beaulieu
52. Provence, The Gordleton Mill, Hordle

53. The Three Lions
    Fordingbridge
54. Chewton Glen, New Milton
55. The Royal Oak Hotel
    Yattendon
56. At The Sign Of The Angel
    Lacock
57. Homewood Park, Bath
58. Hunstrete House,
    Chelwood
59. Blostin's Restaurant,
    Shepton Mallet
60. Maiden Newton House,
    Maiden Newton
61. The Castle Hotel,
    Taunton
62. Whitechapel Manor,
    South Molton
63. Combe House, Gittisham
64. Table Restaurant,
    Babbacombe
65. Gidleigh Park, Chagford
66. The Carved Angel,
    Dartmouth
67. The Abbey Hotel,
    Penzance
68. Susan Hicks

CONTENTS

SOUPS & STARTERS

Fennel and Scallop Mousse

Serves 6

The Mousse:
2 bulbs of fennel
1 small onion
12 scallops
Rind and juice of one lemon
1 oz butter
2 whole eggs and 2 egg whites
¼ pint chicken stock
Seasoning
Double cream

The Sauce:
¼ pint fish stock
¼ pint dry white wine
¼ pint double cream
2 oz butter
12 lightly poached scallops
Julienne of small leek, blanched

The Mousse: Slice fennel and onion and sweat in butter and lemon juice until soft. Add scallops for final minute then chicken stock and bring to the boil, remove from heat. Blend in liquidiser then pass through fine sieve, make up to one pint by adding double cream. Beat the two whole eggs and two egg whites and add to mixture. Pour into buttered or non-stick moulds, place in bain-marie and cook in low oven for 30 minutes until just set.

The Sauce: Reduce stock and wine by half, add cream, then for 30 seconds only add the leek and scallops. Finish with butter and then seasoning.

Stephen and Penny Ross
Homewood Park Hotel
Hinton Charterhouse
Bath
Avon

Asparagus Mousse

1 lb trimmed asparagus
½ pint double cream
4 egg yolks
seasoning
lemon juice
chopped mint (optional)

Cook the well-prepared asparagus ensuring that only tender parts are used.
Cool, chop and place in the liquidiser. Blend until very smooth with the
egg yolks and gradually pour in half-pint of double cream. Add a few drops
of lemon juice. Season with salt and freshly-ground white pepper. Pour
into greased individual dariole moulds and cook in a bain-marie until set.

This mousse is good served cold with smoked prawns or hot with a main
course or simply as a starter with a chervil sauce. Garnish with a few
asparagus spears.

Stephen Smith
The Belvedere Hotel
19 North Park Road
Bradford
West Yorkshire

Smoked Mackerel Mousse with Orange

Serves 6-8

4 Smoked Mackerel
3 egg whites
1 tablespoon tomato puree
¾ pint whipping cream
Nutemeg (pinch)
1 level desssertspoon gelatine (dissolved)
(1 oz flour, 1oz margarine, ½ pint milk, bechamel sauce)
Rind and juice of 1 orange.

De-bone the mackerel. Grate orange and add juice and nutmeg. Make
bechamel sauce and add the tomato puree at end. Stir in the gelatine and
allow to cool. Put the mackerel, orange juice and bechamel sauce in a
blender. Whip cream and fold in. Beat egg whites and fold in.

Sue and Barry Davies
Salisbury House Restaurant
84 Victoria Road
Diss
Norfolk

Mallard Duck Mousse

Two mallard breast
3 fl oz game sauce
one egg
2 fl oz Madeira
2 shallots
salt and pepper
½ pint of whipping cream (approximately)

Blend in food processor, duck breasts with cold sauce, until smooth.
Saute shallots and add Madeira.
Cook out for a few minutes.
Cool slightly then add to blended mixture.
Blend again.
Pass through a medium sieve.
Put into a cold bowl and add a sprinkling of salt and the egg.
Allow to cool in refrigerator.
When cold, beat with a wooden spoon until stiff.
Begin to add the cream until correct consistency is reached.
Test mixture for texture and seasoning. Add more cream and seasoning if necessary.
When complete, place into clingfilmed moulds. Place in a bain-marie and cook in a low oven until set, approximately 15 minutes.

Ramon Farthing
Calcot Manor
Near Tetbury
Gloucestershire

Mushroom Mousse

Serves 4

2 oz finely chopped wild mushrooms
1 tablespoon creme fraiche
1 egg
seasoning
turned mushrooms for garnish

Work all ingredients together and place in moulds lined with cling film.
Steam for 9 minutes.

TASTE BEFORE COOKING - SEASONING

Nick Buckingham
Cavendish Hotel
Baslow
Derbyshire

Chicken Mousse

Stuffed with walnuts and served with a blue Wenslydale dressing

6 oz chicken breast
2 egg yolks
½ pint double cream
2 oz walnuts
1 small onion
2 sticks celery
¼ lb blue Wensleydale
½ pint whipping cream
salt and pepper

Skin the chicken. Roughly dice and puree in the processor until smooth. Add the salt and pepper. Blend and add the egg yolks individually. Scrape down the sides of the bowl to incorporate the mixture thoroughly and pass through a sieve. Chill for an hour.

Meanwhile, finely dice the onion and celery. Sweat in a little butter until soft. Add the chopped walnuts. Season and cool. Carefully beat in the chilled double cream to the puree. Lightly butter four dariole moulds. Half fill with the mixture and spoon in some walnut stuffing. Top with more mousse.

It is better to pipe the mousse in to your moulds thus avoiding air holes when the mousse is cooked. Bake in a bain-marie in a moderate oven until set, covering loosely with tinfoil.

To make the dressing, reduce one quarter of a pint of well-flavoured chicken or vegetable stock by half. Pour in the whipped cream and simmer until it begins to thicken. Crumble in the cheese and stir in until melted. Season with freshly ground pepper.

When the mousses are set, allow to rest out of the oven for three minutes. Turn out onto a serving tray. Surround or pour over with the sauce. Garnish with a spring of herb.

Stephen Smith
The Belvedere Hotel
19 North Park Road
Bradford
West Yorkshire

Smoked Trout Mousse

Serves 4

4 oz smoked pink trout, cleaned and all bones removed. Chill
7 fl oz double cream
ground white pepper
salt if needed
squeeze of lemon juice
1 small bunch garden chives

Place the prepared trout (which has been roughly diced) in the processor and blend until well broken.

Add the cream and lemon juice to the trout and turn on the machine for approximately one minute. Do not over blend otherwise the mixture may curdle.

Remove from the processor and pass through a fine sieve. Taste. Correct the seasoning.

Place in appropriate lined moulds and place in refrigerator until needed.

When serving always remove from fridge before needed to allow the mousse to reach room temperature.

Butter Sauce for Trout Mousse

3 tablespoon white wine
3 tablespoon Noilly Prat
3 tablespoon fish stock
½ lb unsalted butter
3 tablespoon cream

Reduce white wine, Noilly Prat and fish stock by two thirds.

Add cream, boil for two to three minutes.

Whisk in diced up butter.

Boil, season and then liquidise.

Serve warm.

Robert Elsmore
Hunstrete House
Hunstrete
Chelwood
Near Bristol
Avon

Red Pepper Mousse

Makes approximately 12 mousses

1   medium onion (roughly chopped)
3   cloves garlic
8   red peppers
10 ml olive oil
2   tablsp tomato puree
5   whole tomatoes
8   leaves gelatine
3   sprigs basil
1   sprig thyme
¼ pt white wine
½ pt water
salt, pepper, cayenne

Sweat the onion, garlic and peppers in olive oil until soft.

Soak gelatine leaves in cold water.

Add the remaining ingredients to the onion, peppers and garlic and simmer for ½ hour (with a lid on).

Add gelatine.

Puree mixture in a blender.

Pass through a fine sieve.

Season if necessary.

Cling film moulds and pour in the mixture. Refrigerate until set.

N.B. These will keep for up to 4 days in a 'fridge.

Chris Oakes
Oakes Restaurant
169 Slad Road
Stroud
Gloucestershire

Watercress Mousse

Makes 9

½ lb full fat cream cheese
¼ pint lightly whipped double cream
3 tablespoons mayonnaise
3-4 drops tabasco
3 bunches of watercress
1 sachet gelatine
¼ pint chicken stock

Oil medium sized ramekin dishes.
Put cream cheese, mayonnaise, tabasco and watercress leaves into food
processor. Process to a puree.
Melt gelatine in chicken stock.
Whip cream.
Add stock and gelatine and cream to processor. Give machine 2 short spins
and pour into ramekins.
Leave to set (3 hours or more) turn out and serve.
(Freezes very well).

Bryan and Elizabeth Ferriss
Maiden Newton House
Maiden Newton
Nr Dorchester
Dorset

Asparagus Mousse

½ lb fresh asparagus
½ pint bechamel sauce
3 whole eggs
seasoning

Cook the asparagus well, cut into pieces and liquidise with the sauce and
eggs.
Put the mixture into buttered ramekins and cook in hot oven for 10 - 15
minutes.
Serve immediately with a topping of Hollandaise Sauce.

Hollandaise Sauce

½ lb melted butter
3 egg yolks
1 teasp. lemon juice. (or a reduction of white wine vinegar and
                        peppercorns)

Glyn Green
The Abbey Hotel
Abbey Street
Penzance
Cornwall

Mousseline de Coquilles St. Jacques Forestiere

Serves 8

16 fresh scallops
250 ml double cream
1 egg white
a good pinch of salt to taste
freshly ground white pepper

Sauce: 40ml Madeira
       225ml fish stock
       120ml double cream
       225g chilled unsalted butter

Garnish: small selection wild mushrooms (e.g. cepes, oyster mushrooms and chanterelle)

Remove scallops from shell. To clean shell place them in a hot oven and then under cold tap and let soak. Clean the scallop flesh under cold running water being careful not to bruise the flesh. Place the scallop meat in a food processor, along with the salt, and blend until a smooth paste. Add the egg white and mix again thoroughly. Pass through a fine sieve into a bowl set over crushed ice. Mix the cream and white pepper with a spatula (folding method). Taste mousse for seasoning and add more cream if necessary.

Butter the shells on the inside. Dress (fold in) the mousse into the shell which will act as a mould. Once each shell is filled cover it with foil and cook in shallow tray with water (1-2 inches) oven gas mark 5 for 12 minutes.

Sauce - Reduce Madeira until syrupy, then add the fish stock and reduce again. Add cream and reduce to one third consistency, add gradually the butter, lightly stirring the contents until all the butter has melted. Add touch of salt. Lightly stir fry the mushrooms, season and drain ready for garnishing.

To serve - Tip the mousses out of the shells, place just off the centre of each plate and pour a little sauce around them. Sprinkle the sauce with the mushrooms.

Olivier Hubert
"La Bonne Franquette"
5 High Street
Egham
Surrey

Smoked Salmon Pate

½ lb smoked salmon pieces
2 oz butter
1 tablespoon olive oil
2 tablespoon lemon juice
4 tablespoon double cream
½ teaspoon cayenne pepper

Put butter and oil in food processor and cream together, then add salmon
pieces until ground up. Add lemon juice and blend again. Add cream and
cayenne pepper - blend until smooth.

Oliver P Godfrey
Le Grandgousier
15 Western Street
Brighton
Sussex

Stilton and Walnut Pate

Grate 12 oz Stilton into mixing bowl. Add 4 small or 2 large blocks of
Philadelphia cheese, mix together with a fork.

Melt 4 oz unsalted butter and add to the mixture, add 3 tablespoons of port
and a handful of chopped parsley. Break up 3 oz of walnuts and add to the
mixture.

Turn into lined pate dish.

Lorna Levis
At the Sign of the Angel
Lacock
Wiltshire

Pancake Pate Slice

Five 7 inch (18cm) thin pancakes

For the Mushroom Pate:

2 oz (60g) butter
4 oz (120g) minced onions
1 lb (480g) minced mushrooms
½ pint (275 ml) red wine
salt and freshly ground black pepper
Marsala

For the Chicken Liver Pate:

¾ lb (360g) chicken livers
4 oz (120g) butter
1 small chopped onion
1 clove crushed garlic
salt and freshly ground black pepper

To make the mushroom pate:
Melt the butter in a large saucepan over a gently heat, add minced onions
and simmer for about ten minutes. Add mushrooms, salt and pepper and stir
well. Add red wine and simmer slowly over a low heat, stirring
occasionally until the liquid evaporates, and the mixture is dry. This
will take at least one hour. Cool. Add a little Marsala to the mixture.

To make the chicken liver pate:
Put the chicken livers, butter, onion and garlic in a roasting tin, into a
hot oven until the livers are cooked (but still slightly pink in the
centre). Liquidise. Season. Cool.

To assemble the gateau:
Put the first pancake onto a large plate, and spread onto it half the
mushroom pate mixture. On top of this place another pancake and then
spread onto this half the chicken liver pate. Repeat this process
finishing up with a pancake.

This slice will serve either eight as a starter or four as a main course.
My suggested accompaniment is a crisp, crunchy salad made up of finely-
sliced red cabbage, chopped celery, bean sprouts and finely-sliced Chinese
cabbage tossed in a vinaigrette dressing.

Joy Hadley
Rumbles Cottage Restaurant
Braintree Road
Felstead
Essex

Rillettes de Volaille et de Truite Fumees au Raifort

Coarse pate of smoked chicken and smoked pink river trout served with a whipped horseradish sauce.

Serves 4

250g (¼) smoked chicken
1 smoked pink river trout
60g butter, softened,
1 tomato, blanched, skinned, deseeded and chopped
1 tblsp capers
1 tsp fresh parsley, finely chopped
½ tsp Dijon mustard
½ juice lemon

Horseradish Cream

Mixed together:
        10 cl whipped cream
        1 tsp horseradish sauce

Bone the trout and ¼ chicken, cut them in small pieces.
Mix thoroughly all other ingredients in a bowl (butter, tomato, capers, parsley, mustard and lemon juice).
Add the smoked trout and chicken and mix until the preparation is quite sticky.
Serve with some of the horseradish cream and as a decoration some curly endive, a drop of olive oil vinaigrette and a little of red fish roe.

This tasty starter demands 20 minutes preparation with NO COOKING AT ALL.
It can be prepared in advance as we do not use fresh trout and fresh chicken and keeps very well in the 'fridge.
Served with brown toast or French baguette.

We recommend as a perfect companion a Gaillac Perle, Domaine Jean Cros 86. A fresh, lively dry white wine with a faint sparkle from the North-East or Toulouse in the South of France.

Regis Crepy
The Great House Hotel and Restaurant
Market Place
Lavenham
Suffolk

Filo Baskets of Mussels with Bacon and Brie

Serves 6

Baskets:

18 x 15 cm sq sheets filo pastry

Layer three squares of filo with each successive sheet turned through 30 degrees and brushed with clarified butter. This forms an eleven-pointed star shape. Ease the star shape into a buttered No 1 ramekin, sides facing down and the points of the star facing up. Push down well and prick the bottom with a fork. Repeat for other five baskets. Bake for six minutes at gas mark 5. Remove from oven, lift baskets out of ramekins. Turn upside down and replace in oven on baking sheet for further two minutes until evenly brown. Leave to cool on a wire rack.

Mussel filling:

5 lb mussels, rinsed, scrubbed and debearded
1 onion, finely chopped
2 cloves garlic, crushed and finely chopped
2 oz butter
5 fl oz double cream
15 fl oz reserved mussel juice
10 fl oz dry white wine
juice of ½ lemon
salt, fresh ground pepper and pinch of sugar
6 oz smoked back bacon, grilled, drained and finely sliced
3 oz ripe Brie

Open mussels in a hot, dry pan with tight fitting lid. Do not overcook. Drain in colander and set over a bowl. Shell mussels and strain juice carefully through double muslin. Sweat onions and garlic in butter. Add stock, white wine and reduce by ¾. Add lemon juice, cream and seasoning and reduce until very thick. Add bacon and mussels and heat through. Pile mixture into filo baskets; top with a square of brie and melt under grill. Serve of a plate surrounded by dressed salad leaves, herbs and diced tomato.

Mr and Mrs N Nairn
Braeval Old Mill Restaurant
by Aberfoyle
Stirlingshire
Scotland

Ravioli De Morille Au Fumet De Mousseron

Serves 4

15 pieces of ravioli per person

Ravioli pasta:
1 kg flour
6 whole eggs
18 egg yolks
400 gr duxelle of mushrooms
30 pre-cooked morilles

Sauce:
4 dl chicken stock
2 dl white wine
4 dl cream
120gr mousserons

Pasta:
Mix together the flour, egg yolks and whole eggs, and form dough into a ball. Roll the pasta as thin as possible and cut 120 circles 5cm in diameter.
Place 60 rounds of pasta on the table and place the duxelle of mushrooms on each one together with half a morille. Cover each with the remaining 60 circles of pasta making sure they are well sealed.

Sauce:
Reduce the white wine and chicken stock by half. Add the mousserons and cream and cook until the correct consistency is reached. Season to taste.

Presentation:
Cook the ravioli in boiling water for about 5-6 minutes. Place on plates and add sauce over the top. Serve very hot.

Pierre Chevillard
Chewton Glen Hotel
New Milton
Hampshire

Flan D'Asperges et Morrilles Farcie au Gratin

Serves 4

4 flan cases
200g mixed wild mushrooms
30g shallots
10g garlic
60g butter
100g asparagus
10cl brandy
20cl chicken stock
20cl double cream

5cl tomato coulis
1 egg yolk
5cl whipped cream
10cl mustard sauce
15g chopped mixed herbs
30g butter to finish
picked basil

Place some butter in a pan and saute the shallots and garlic together.
Add the wild mushrooms and asparagus and season with salt and pepper.
Deglace with the brandy and reduce by one half.
Remove the vegetables to stop them over cooking and keep warm.
Reduce the excess liquor further down and then gradually add the chicken
stock until it is a thick sticky liquid.
Add the double cream and check the seasoning and consistency.
Line the flan case with a little tomato coulis.
Place the egg into the sauce and pass through a fine sieve.
Add the cream and mushrooms along with the asparagus and fold together.
Place in the flan case and glaze.
Mount the mustard sauce with some butter and infuse with the herbs.
Place the flan sauce upon the sauce and garnish with the picked basil.
Serve immediately

Alan J Hill
The Gleneagles Hotel
Auchterarder
Perthshire
Scotland

Gateau of Green Tomato

600g green tomato juice
1 tablespoon olive oil
juice of 1 lemon
100g juice of sorrel
8 leaves of gelatine
salt and pepper
400g cream
6 egg whites

Line mould with carrot, turnip, swede and celeriac.
Liquidise tomatoes, olive oil, lemon juice.
Pass through a sieve.
Bring to the boil, remove and add a little cornflour.
Add gelatine.
When cooled semi-whip cream and season.
Incorporate whites, add half tomatoes, mix cream.
Add the rest of the tomatoes plus sorrel juice.
Mould.

Kevin Cape
The Bell Inn
Aston Clinton
Buckinghamshire

Avocado and Prawn Cheesecake

Melt 100g of butter and stir in 1 packet of crushed cheddar cheese biscuits. Use to line base of 20cm springclip cake tin.

Dissolve 11g of gelatine in 6 tblsp of water. In food processor puree 2 large avocados with the juice of 1 large lemon. Once smooth add 3 egg yolks and 225g of cream cheese and process again. Add salt and freshly ground black pepper to taste. Transfer mixture to a large bowl, fold in gelatine and place in 'fridge until on the point of setting. Whisk 3 egg whites until stiff and fold in to avocado mixture. Pour half of the mixture on to the biscuit base, add one pound of peeled prawns, and then pour on remaining mixture. Put back in the 'fridge to set.

Joy Hadley
Rumbles Cottage Restaurant
Braintree Road
Felstead
Essex

Stir Fry Squid

Serves 1

2 oz sunflower oil
1 clove of garlic
½ fresh chilli fried in the oil (do not serve the cilli)
a little ginger puree
4 oz prepared squid
1 oz sliced spring onions
1 oz carrot diamonds
1 oz beansprouts
2 oz fish stock with 1 tblsp light soy sauce, ½ teaspoon cornflour
roasted flaked peanuts and chives.

In a wok heat the oil and fry the garlic, ginger and chilli (one minute)
ADD THE DRY SQUID AND FRY 1 MINUTE.
Stir in the vegetables add the stock and cook until it thickens, serve in a bowl with nut and chive sprinkled on the top.

WITH THE SOY SAUCE AND CHILLI YOU SHOULD NOT NEED ANY SEASONING BUT CHECK JUST THE SAME.

Nick Buckingham
Cavendish Hotel
Baslow
Derbyshire

Prawn and Parmesan Fritters

For Choux pastry:

> 12 fl oz water
> 4 oz butter or margarine
> 5½ oz plain flour
> 3-4 eggs
> salt

2 oz grated parmesan
8 oz peeled prawns
dash of Tabasco or pinch of Cayenne
Mill-pepper

Place water in saucepan with salt and butter and bring to the boil.
Add sieved flour and beat in thoroughly with wooden spoon until mixture
leaves sides of pan clean. Remove from heat.
Allow to cool for a few minutes and then beat in eggs one at a time until a
dripping consistency is reached.
Beat in parmesan and seasonings and then fold in peeled prawns.
Spoon fritters on to greased greaseproof paper, then fry in 'Friteuse' at
350 deg F until golden brown - serve immediately.

C E Oakely
The Pier At Harwich
The Quay
Harwich
Essex

Souffle Suissesse
(Souffles with Swiss cheese)

This is an original way of serving a cheese souffle; the cheese is not incorporated into the souffle mixture but is used to glaze it. Nevertheless, it is a light dish with a wonderful aroma, which has delighted diners at Le Gavroche since the day we opened. As they cook, the souffles will absorb the cream and will be very rich and creamy.

Serves 4

140g (5oz) butter
65g (2oz) flour
700ml (28fl oz) milk
5 egg yolks
1L (1¾pts) double cream
6 egg whites
200g (7oz) grated Gruyere or Emmental cheese
salt
freshly ground white pepper

Preparation time: 25 minutes
Cooking time: 8 minutes

Wine: with this creamy sauce, serve a light Pouilly Fuisse.

The Souffle mixture: Preheat the oven to 200oC/400oF/Gas 6.

Melt 65g (2oz) butter in a small saucepan set over low heat. Using a small wire whisk, stir in the flour. Cook gently for 2 or 3 minutes, stirring continuously.

Take the pan off the heat and leave the roux to cool slightly. Bring the milk to the boil, then pour it over the cooled roux, whisking all the time. Set the pan over high heat and, stirring continuously, bring the mixture to the boil and cook for 3 minutes.

Take the pan off the heat and stir in the egg yolks. Season to taste with salt and pepper. Dot the surface with 1 tblsp. butter, cut into small pieces, to prevent a skin from forming. Set aside at room temperature.

Meanwhile, chill 8 round 8cm (3in) tartlet tins in the refrigerator or freezer for a few minutes. Remove and immediately grease them generously with softened butter and arrange on a baking sheet.

Assembling the Souffles: Pour the cream into a gratin or bi-metal dish. Lightly salt the cream, then warm it gently without letting it boil. Beat the egg whites with a pinch of salt until they form stiff peaks. Pour the souffle mixture into a wide-mouthed bowl. Using a whisk, quickly beat in about one-third of the beaten egg whites, then, using a spatula, carefully fold in the remainder. Using a tablespoon, heap up the mixture in the tartlet tins to form 8 large mounds.

To Cook and Serve: Bake the souffles in the preheated oven for 3 minutes, until the tops begin to turn golden. Remove from the oven and, protecting your hands with a cloth, turn out each souffle into the dish of warm cream. Sprinkle over the Gruyere or Emmental and return to the oven for 5 minutes.

The souffles must be taken immediately to the table; serve them with a spoon and fork, taking care not to crush them.

Albert Roux
Le Gavroche
Upper Brook Street
London

Haddock Souffle

8 oz smoked haddock
2 oz prawns
1 oz butter
1 oz flour
1/3rd pint milk
lemon juice
3 large eggs (separated)
Parmesan cheese

Melt butter and then stir in flour. Remove from heat and blend in milk, lemon juice and seasoning.
Return to heat. Stir in egg yolks and fish.
Beat egg whites and fold into mix.
Add Parmesan cheese.
Bake in oven for 25 minutes, gas mark 5, electric 190.

Steven P Saunders
The Pink Geranium
Melbourn
Royston
Hertfordshire

26

Souffle aux Epinards, Sauce Anchois

Serves 6

For the Souffle:

75gms	Flour
75gms	Butter
600ml	Milk, infused with onion, bay leaf, clove and heated
4	Eggs, separated
100gms	Spinach, washed (leaves only)
	Cayenne
	Ground Nutmeg
	Salt

For the Sauce:

1 tblsp	Water
3	Egg yolks
225gms	Clarified butter (i.e. melted butter with the milky residue removed)
1 sml tin	Anchovy fillets, squeezed free from oil
Cayenne	
Salt	
Lemon juice to taste	

Preheat the oven to gas mark 4 (180oC/350oF).

Make a roux by melting the butter and adding flour. Cook slowly and do not allow it to colour. Add the infused milk (which has been strained) to the roux gradually, stirring constantly, making sure there are no lumps. When all the milk has been added, allow to cook out slowly (this will take approximately 15 minutes).

Cook the spinach in a little boiling salted water and refresh in cold water. Squeeze thoroughly and chop finely.

Add a pinch of salt to the egg whites and beat up until very stiff.

Season the sauce with cayenne, nutmeg and salt. Add egg yolks and mix thoroughly. Add spinach, continuing to mix and fold in, little by little, the beaten egg whites.

Fill 6 well-buttered individual souffle moulds and cook in oven for about 20 minutes. Serve with the sauce.

To make the sauce:

Add the tablespoon of water to the egg yolks. Cook over a gentle heat,
whisking continuously to a sabayon (a mixture of egg yolks and a little
water, whisked to the ribbon stage in a double saucepan). Allow to cool
slightly and slowly add the warm clarified butter. When combined, add a
little cayenne,salt and a squeeze of lemon jiuce. Blend the anchovy
fillets with a drop of water to a smooth paste. Put into a bowl, add
sauce, whisking continuously until thoroughly mixed. Pass through a fine
chinois and serve with the souffles.

Richard Shepherd
Langans Brasserie
Stratton Street
Piccadilly,
London

Avocado Salad dressed with Garlic Croutons and Crispy Bacon

Serves 4

1 avocado (large)
8 oz assorted French lettuces
 (available from most large supermarkets already mixed)
2 fl oz vinaigrette dressing
2 slices of thick white bread
1 clove garlic
2 slices back bacon
2 oz butter

Toss salad in vinaigrette and place in the centre of four plates.
Take rind off bacon and discard, cut into strips of about $\frac{1}{4}$ inch wide and
place in saucepan with cold water, bring to the boil and refresh in cold
water, strain and put aside.
Cut crusts off bread and discard, but into $\frac{1}{4}$ inch dice, crush garlic, place
butter in hot pan and add bread then garlic and fry until golden brown and
put aside.
Peel avocado and cut into quarters, slice each quarter into about 6 slices
and arrange around the salad.
Put bacon in a frying pan and brown, add croutons of bread.
Sprinkle bacon and croutons over salad and serve.

John Mann
The Montagu Arms Hotel
Beaulieu
Hampshire

Twice Baked Stilton and Garlic Souffle

Serves 10 - 12

1½ oz butter	1½ oz flour
10 fl oz milk	12 oz stilton cheese
5 egg yolks	6 egg whites
2 fl oz white wine	2 tablespoons olive oil
3 bulbs of garlic (not cloves)	3 oz cheddar cheese
3 oz wholemeal breadcrumbs	10 fl oz double cream
seasoning.	

Break the garlic into cloves but do not peel.
Put in an earthenware dish with the oil and wine and bake at gas 4/350 deg F for 30 minutes.
Allow the garlic to cool before peeling.
Pass the garlic through a fine sieve - should be 3 tablespoons of puree.

*THIS BASE SAUCE CAN BE MADE IN THE MORNING AND RE-HEATED AT NIGHT.
Melt the butter, stir in the flour and cook out as for a white roux.
Add the milk slowly and allow to thicken over a medium heat.
Cut up the stilton cheese and mix into the sauce, allow to simmer for 5 minutes.
Add the egg yolks to sauce and thicken very gently (do not allow to boil or it will split)
Pass the sauce through a fine strainer and allow to cool. (cover with cling folm to stop a skin forming)

Butter the individual pudding dishes twice (traditional pudding shape if possible)
Fold the garlic puree in to the sauce base and warm over a bain-marie, season.
Whisk the egg whites to the soft peak stage with a little salt.
Fold these into the warm sauce mixture gently.
Fill the pudding dishes and bake in a bain-marie for 35-45 minutes gas 4/350 deg F until firm - loosely cover bain-marie with tin foil.
When the puddings are firm remove from oven and take out of bain-marie, allow to cool.
Turn out the puddings onto individual sur-le-plats (flat oven-proof dishes).
Divide double cream between each souffle by pouring over the top - leaving extra around the bottom for a sauce.
Cover each one with the grated cheddar cheese and breadcrumbs.
Bake for 15 minutes at gas 6/400 deg F in the middle of the oven.
Take out when golden brown - garnish with a sprig of chervil and serve immediately.

Colin John Bussey
The Gleneagles Hotel
Auchterarder
Perthshire

Gravad Lax (Marinated Fresh Salmon)

Serves: 4 - 3oz marinated salmon as hors d'oevre
       2 - 6oz marinated salmon as main course

Marinating salmon:

to each pound of salmon add:

1 oz salt
1 oz sugar
pinch saltpetre
5 white peppercorns, crushed
3 juniper berries, crushed
plenty of dill or spruce twigs

Salmon is best for marinating in spring. If possible select a middle cut.
Scrape the salmon and dry it thoroughly with a cloth, but do not rinse the
fish. Slit the salmon open along the backbone and take it out, pulling out
any small bones with pliers or tweezers. Mix the salt, sugar and saltpetre
together and rub the mixture into the salmon. Put a layer of fresh dill or
spruce twigs (if available) into a shallow dish. Put one half of the
salmon on top with the skin side downwards. Sprinkle the fish with plently
of dill together with the crushed peppercorns and juniper berries. Place
other half of salmon on top with the skin side uppermost. Cover the salmon
with dill or spruce twigs. Put a weighted choppingboard or similar on top
of the salmon and leave in a cool, dark place for 48 hours. The salmon is
then ready to serve and can be stored for a week or more if kept in a cold
place.

After scraping off the spices and herbs from the fish, the salmon may be
served in thin slices or in portion-sized pieces. Thin slices are cut
obliquely or vertically and are served spread out in a single layer, folded
double or rolled up. Portion-sized pieces are cut into steaks.

The skin may be cut into strips, fried and served with the salmon. Garnish
with fresh dill and serve with a dressing of oil, vinegar, sweet mustard,
white pepper, salt, sugar and chopped dill. Alternatively, serve the
marinated salmon and the ingredients for the dressing separately, the
dressing then being made at the table as required. The salmon may also be
served with creamed or sauted potatoes, sauted spinach, poached eggs or new
boiled potatoes.

Karl Wadsack
The Three Lions
Stuckton
Fordingbridge
Hampshire

Stuffed Endive with Prawns and Leeks

4 Belgian endives (chicory)
½ lb peeled prawns
2 leeks
2 dl double cream
2 dl white wine (dry)
½ lemon
butter

Cook whole endives in simmering salted water, with ½ lemon added, for 5 minutes. Remove and drain, allow to cool.

Finely chop cleaned leeks and sweat with a little butter until soft. Add wine and reduce to a trace. Add cream and reduce until thick. Season. Peel away, gently, the leaves of the endives and arrange, on to four small plates, as petals of a flower, overlapped slightly. Add prawns to leek mixture and spoon into the centre of each flower. Lift up 'petals' to envelop the filling and fasten with a cocktail stick at the top, to keep parcel in shape. Cover each with foil and cook in oven gas 3 for 30 minutes until hot. Remove cocktail stick and foil and serve.
Sauce with a beurre blanc or a white wine fish sauce if liked.

T J Brooks
Table Restaurant
135 Babbacombe Road
Babbacombe
Devon

Hot Crab Ramekin

Serves 4/6 depending on size of ramekin.

1 lb crab meat (freshly picked if possible and drain any liquid)
1 cup thick double cream
grated cheese
anchovy essence
chilli sauce

Mix cream and crab meat together over gentle heat. Add a little grated cheese, a pinch of dried mustard powder or mace, a drop of lemon juice and some anchovy essence and chilli sauce. Grate in plenty of ground pepper and a pinch of salt and heat until hot. Pour into ramekin dishes and sprinkle with grated cheese. Brown under the grill or in a hot oven.

NB To make the mixture less rich a cheese sauce may be used instead of cream. The mixture can be made before and heated in the oven or a microwave before browning.

Nicholas and Nicola Hayward
Seaview Hotel and Restaurant
The High Street
Seaview
Isle of Wight

Cocktail De Truite Fumee A L'Avocat

Serves 4

2 Avocados
320g smoked trout
20g salmon roe
fresh chive
20 crushed coriander seeds
lemon juice
worcester sauce
20dl whipped cream
salad for decoration

Peel the avocado and then cut into small cubes. Cut the trout the same size. Mix the trout, avocado, the chopped chive and the coriander seeds together.

Whip the cream but not too firmly (just enough to bind ingredients) add salt and pepper to taste, a little worcester sauce and lemon juice. Add ingredients and salmon roe to the cream and fold in.

Serve on a bed of salad.

Claire and Jean Pierre Novi
The Gordelton Mill
Silver Street
Hordle
Nr Lymington
Hampshire

Gravadlax of Salmon

In a basin mix:

8 oz course sea salt
8 oz dried dill weed
8 oz demerara sugar

soak with brandy until mix feels like wet sand.

Descale and fillet one whole salmon, remove all small bones and lay skin side down on a sheet of tin foil, cover salmon with mixture and close fillets together, wrap tightly in cling film and then lay in leakproof container and top with a heavy weight. i.e. a chopping board. Leave for at least three days, turn every twelve hours.

The Head Chef
Rogano
Seafood Bar and Restaurant
11 Exchange Place
Glasgow

Champignons aux Fleurs de Courgette en Persillade

Serves 4

600g of assorted wild mushrooms, e.g. girolles, oyster,
    saint george
20 courgette flowers
3 cloves garlic
100g parsley
50g butter
1dl double cream

Blanch the flowers in boiling water, remove from water and cool in ice water.

Wash the mushrooms, chop the garlic and parsley finely. Warm some oil in a pan and fry the mushrooms for 1 minute. Drain the mushrooms and then fry again, this time in a gentle heat with the butter. Add salt, pepper, garlic and the parsley and continue cooking for 3 minutes.

Put a quarter of the mushrooms in food processor and add the cream. Mix only for a short time, the mushrooms should not be too fine.

Fill a piping bag with the mushrooms and stuff the flowers. Put the stuffed flowers in an oven dish and cook for 4 minutes.

Serve on a bed of the remaining mushrooms.

Claire and Jean Pierre Novi
The Gordelton Mill
Silver Street
Hordle
Nr Lymington
Hampshire

Pear and Prosciutto

Allow ½ Pear per person

Peel the pear, halve and scoop out the stalk and core. Squeeze lemon juice on so it does not discolour. Slice thinly and arrange in a fan on side of plate. Spoon on a little vinaigrette making sure the pear is covered. Sprinkle on parsley and 3 or 4 black olives. Arrange prosciutto on other side of plate.
Vinaigrette: salt, pepper, mustard, honey, a little garlic, white wine vinegar, oil, ½ olive and ½ grape or peanut oil.

Oliver P Godfrey
Le Grandgousier
15 Western Street
Brighton
Sussex

Gazpacho

Gazpacho is a chilled summer soup prepared from salad vegetables. It originates from Spain and is often referred to as Gazpacho Andalucia. An ideal first course for warm days especially when dining 'al fresco'. An added bonus is that it is supposed to be very good if you are suffering from a hangover.

1½ lbs (600g) ripe tomatoes
4 oz (100g) sliced onions
1 cucumber
1 red pepper
1 green pepper
1 clove garlic
4 oz (100g) dried bread
4 fl oz (100ml) olive oil
4 fl oz (100ml) white wine vinegar
1½ pints (½ litre) cold water
salt and pepper to taste

Peel the onion, cucumber and garlic and slice thinly.
Cut the peppers in half, remove the seeds and slice.
Quarter the tomatoes and add the remainder of the ingredients.
Allow the soup to marinate for at least one hour in a refrigerator before liquidizing.
Serve in chilled soup bowls of your choice with the following garnish.

Garnish
½ cucumber
4 tomatoes
½ large Spanish onion
½ red pepper
½ green pepper
4 slices of white bread

Peel the cucumber and remove the seeds, cut into dice.
Blanch, skin and seed the tomatoes and dice the flesh.
Peel the onion and finely chop.
Remove the seeds from the peppers and dice.
Remove the crusts from the bread, cut into cubes and fry in clarified butter.
Serve the garnish in six separate bowls for your guests to help themselves at service time.

David and Rona Pitchford
Read's
Painter's Forstal
Faversham
Kent

35

Redberry Soup

A soup for high summer.

Serves 4

½ bottle red wine
¼ bottle port
½ a cinnamon stick
80g caster sugar
1 mill fresh ground black pepper

Soft fruit - any soft summer fruits

e.g. Strawberries, Raspberries, Redcurrants, Blackcurrants,
     Blueberries, Loganberries, Blackberries, Wild Strawberries.
     Sufficient for four people.

Mix all ingredients, except the fruit.
Heat in a saucepan to infuse the cinnamon and dissolve the sugar.
Heat but DO NOT BOIL.
Allow liquid to cool, then pass through a fine sieve.
Add the fresh fruit.
Refrigerate - preferably for 1 - 2 days to allow fruit to marinate.

Stuart Busby
Heath Lodge Hotel
Danesbury Park Road
Welwyn
Hertfordshire

Cream of Pumpkin Soup with Cheese Croutons

3 lb pumpkin	salt and pepper
1½ lb onions	2 pints of milk, boiled
2 sticks celery	1½ pints of chicken stock

Sweat the finely diced onions and celery in a little butter, add the diced pumpkin flesh, removing the seeds and cottony centre, cover with the milk and stock, season. Simmer until soft about 35 to 40 minutes. Puree the mixture in the liquidiser, check for seasoning adding a few drops of lemon juice to "lift" the soup. Serve hot with a little cream, top with a cheese crouton sprinkled with parsley or chives.

Stephen Smith
The Belvedere Hotel
19 North Park Road
Bradford
West Yorkshire

Tourin D'ail

(Garlic Soup)

3 lb (1.5kg) chicken winglets and giblets (no Livers)
4 heads garlic
1 cup white wine
2 carrots, 1 celeriac (or ½ head celery), and white
  part of 2 leeks, finely chopped.
3 sprigs thyme, 1 bay leaf, 2 sprigs parsley and
  1 sprig tarragon.
Salt and ¼ teasp. black pepper
4 pints (2.25L) water
2 egg yolks
¼ pint (150ml) cream

Brown the chicken pieces, preferably in goose/duck fat or olive oil, then
add the chopped vegetables and stir until softened. Add the wine, water,
herbs and seasoning and simmer for 2 hours. Remove from heat, sieve and
skim off excess fat.

Break up the garlic heads and peel each clove by tapping sharply with a
flat weight (most of the skin will fall off): do not use a knife. Gently
simmer the garlic in the soup for 1 hour. Liquidise and keep hot, adding
salt to taste.

Just before serving, beat together the egg yolks and cream, and pour into
soup, stirring continuously.

Nicholas Blacklock
La Bastide
50 Greek Street
London

Hollandaise Soup

½ cucumber
2 small carrots
1 small turnip
2 oz fresh or frozen peas
fresh or dried tarragon
2 egg yolks
½ pint cream
2 pints chicken stock
seasoning
2 oz butter
2 oz flour

Chop vegetables in uniform cubes or slices (small).
Place butter in pan and melt.
Add flour and make a roux.
Add chicken stock, stirring all the time until thickened.
Add prepared vegetables - not the peas if frozen.
Bring to the boil and cook until the vegetables are cooked.

Beat egg yolks and cream together and add this as a liaison to the soup.
Do not let it boil or else a curdling effect will take place.
Add tarragon and just let it sit on a warm heat, also add the parsley.
The flavour of the tarragon should come through but if this has not
happened, add just a little tarragon vinegar.
Season to taste.

Francis Coulson and Brian Sack
Sharrow Bay Country House Hotel
Lake Ullswater
Penrith
Cumbria

Tomato Apple and Celery Soup

1 lb fresh soft tomatoes
8 oz chopped apple
8 oz celery
4 oz onion
2 oz leeks
2 small carrots
1 clove of garlic crushed
chicken stock
dry sherry

Roughly chop all ingredients.

Sweat the onion, leek, carrot and garlic in a little butter till cooked but
not browned.

Add tomatoes, apple and celery, 1 glassful of dry sherry. Bring to the
boil and cover, simmer for 10 minutes add chicken stock, return to boil
then cover and simmer again for approximately 45 minutes till all is soft.

Pass through food processor and sieve or just sieve making sure to press
well.

Adjust seasoning and consistency with stock or cream.

Stephen and Anne Frost
The Stonor Arms
Stonor
Nr Henley-on-Thames
Oxfordshire

Minestrone Soup

Serves 6

We tend to regard minestrone in this country as a watery tomato soup with
funny shaped bits of pasta in it, but in Italy and indeed parts of Greece
and the Balkans as well it is a wonderful mixed vegetable soup make with
whatever ingredients are appropriate at the time. The only things that are

normally common are beans, sometimes fresh and sometimes dry, and some pasta although it comes in various shapes and sizes depending on the region. This is a super minestrone that makes a meal in itself. By the way there are no tomatoes in it so don't be disappointed if it doesn't come out red - it certainly won't be thin.

½lb cooked cannelloni or haricot beans (soak overnight and
              cook for 1½ hours or use a tin)
1 large onion
½ lb each, leeks, carrots and turnips.
half savoy cabbage
4 oz pasta spirals.

Clean and peel all the vegetables. Cut onion, leeks, carrots and turnips into quarter inch dice. Cut the cabbage in half, remove the core and shred across. Put two pints of water in a large saucepan and add a teaspoon of salt. Add the root vegetables, pasta and beans and cook gently again for another 10 minutes and then add the cabbage, bringing to a rapid boil for 3 minutes. Check for seasoning cover and leave to stand for a minute or two for the flavours to blend thoroughly. Serve it in deep bowls with a good generous tablespoon of grated parmesan to sprinkle over the top. Black pepper is usually grated on at the same time as the parmesan. Good chunky, solid Italian style bread is delicious with this especially if it has been preheated in the oven.

Michael Barry

(Michael Barry is probably best known to most people for his appearances on BBC's Food and Drink Programme, he is also the author of several cookery books)

Cullen Skink

Cream of Smoked Haddock Soup

1 lb smoked haddock fillet
1 lb leeks
2 medium onions
1 lb potatoes
4 oz butter or margarine
3 pints chicken stock (stock cubes)
seasoning
¼ pint double cream
whisky

Thoroughly wash leeks and drain well.
Roughly chop onions and leeks.
Melt butter in thick bottomed pan and add onions and leeks - sweat off lightly.
Add chicken stock and bring to boil.
Skin smoked haddock, reserving 4 oz for garnish. Cut remaining haddock into cubes.
Roughly chop peeled potatoes and add with the 12 oz fish to the soup.

Allow to simmer for about ½ hour.
In the meantime lightly poach remaining 4 oz fish, then drain and allow to cool.
Liquidise soup and pass through a sieve.
Correct for seasoning and finish with whisky (to taste), cream and flaked garnish.

C E Oakley
The Pier at Harwich
The Quay
Harwich
Essex

A Clear Tomato Soup with Vegetable Diamonds

Serves 10 - 12

4 lbs ripe tomatoes
12 oz peeled vegetables: onions, leeks, carrots, celery (cut into dice)
sprig of rosemary and one bay leaf
1 peeled clove of garlic
½ pint white wine
1½ pints vegetable stock
1 pint tomato passata or tomato juice
seasoning and celery salt
6 egg whites and shells
vegetable diamonds cut from leeks, red pepper and carrots
chervil

Place all ingredients (except diamonds and chervil) in processor and chop until very fine puree.
Place in pan with stock, wine and tomato passata.
Season with care REMEMBER YOU CAN NOT SEASON AFTER COOKING.
Bring to the boil slowly stirring only once.
Simmer for 20 minutes and stand for 10 minutes.
With great care strain into a very clean pan, the soup through a double chinois fitted with a filter paper.
Reboil the soup and garnish with vegetable diamonds.
At the last minute add some sprigs of chervil.

MAKE SURE THAT THE SOUP IS CLEAR AND BRIGHT
MAKE SURE THAT THE TOMATOES ARE RIPE

Nick Buckingham
Cavendish Hotel
Baslow
Derbyshire

Gaspacho A L'Andalouse

Chilled Tomato and Vegetable soup

Serves 4

200g peeled tomatoes
100g peeled cucumbers
30g onions
30g red pepper
20g greenpepper
½ clove chopped garlic
15g white breadcrumbs
2cl red wine vinegar
5cl poultry stock
4cl olive oil
15g basil
5cl single cream
salt and freshly ground pepper

Chop the tomatoes, cucumber, onions and peppers into small cubes and place
into a large stainless steel bowl.
Add the garlic and breadcrumbs and mix together thoroughly.
Pour in the vinegar and poultry stock and marinade for 24 hours in a
refrigerator
Pour in the hand blender and gradually add olive oil and single cream.
Check the seasoning and keep on ice.
Julienne the basil leaves and add to the soup.
Pour into ice cold soup dishes and serve immediately.

Alan J Hill
The Gleneagles Hotel
Auchterarder
Perthshire
Scotland

Curried Pea Soup

Serves 6

1 onion
1 clove garlic
2 oz margarine or butter
5 oz celery (4 sticks)
3 dessertspoons mild curry powder
½ dessertspoon thyme
½ dessertspoon garam masala
1 dessertspoon coriander
pinch of chilli
1 dessertspoon Tamari (or soy sauce)
2 oz flour
10 oz frozen peas
17 fl oz milk
10½ fl oz stock
1½ fl oz cream

Saute onion and celery in butter with all herbs and spices.
Reduce heat, add flour and make a roux. Cook until it resembles
breadcrumbs.
Add milk, stock and peas.
Blend until smooth. Season and add tamari cream and a sprig of fresh
coriander.

Jane Stimpson
Food For Thought
31 Neal Street
Covent Garden
London WC2

Mushroom and Mustard Soup

2 medium onions   2 carrots
2 medium leeks   1 lb mushrooms
4 sticks celery   1 glass dry sherry
Mustard to taste
Chicken stock or water and stock cube

Roughly chop all vegetables and sweat in 2 oz butter until soft, add
stock/water and cube to cover and sherry.

Bring to the boil, then simmer till all vegetables are soft, approximately
40 minutes. Puree in a liquidiser, adjust seasoning, mustard to taste and
consistency by adding stock or cream.

Stephen and Anne Frost
The Stonor Arms
Stonor
Nr Henley-on-Thames
Oxfordshire

Spring Vegetable Soup

2 tblsp olive oil
½ lb potatoes
2 leeks
2 carrots
¼ lb green beans
(all these must be diced small)
1 lb dried haricot beans (soaked overnight)
3½ pts chicken stock
3 oz dried vermicelli
4 ripe tomatoes, peeled and chopped

Pesto:
4 garlic cloves, crushed
4 heaped tblsp freshly chopped basil

Take the olive oil and sweat the carrots and potatoes off and add small
amount of chicken stock, cook until tender.
Cook haricot beans until tender in small amount of water and chicken stock.
Cook vermicelli on a metal tray.
To serve put all ingredients and chicken stock in pan and simmer for 5
minutes.
Just before you serve put half a teaspoon of pesto in soup.

Brian J Baker
Hambleton Hall
Hambleton
Oakham
Rutland

Cream of Lovage and Sorrel Soup

Serves 6

4 pts jellied chicken stock	½lb peeled and diced potatoes
1 pt double cream	6 oz chopped celery
4 oz garden sorrel	clove garlic
4 oz garden lovage	2 oz butter
1 lb leeks (white part only)	seasoning / nutmeg
6 oz onions, diced	

Melt the butter in a thick bottomed pan and sweat off all the vegetables,
then add the herbs and stock.
Cook for 1-1½ hours, liquidise and pass through a fine sieve.
Season to taste.
Simmer for 20 minutes, add the cream and serve.

Amanda and James Graham
Ostlers Close Restaurant
25 Bonnygate
Cupar
Fife

Mushroom Bisque Soup

Serves 6

12 oz button mushrooms (thinly sliced)
1 onion
1 oz parsley (chopped)
1 large carrot (grated)
1 clove garlic
2 dessertspoons tomato puree
7 fl oz white wine
3½ fl oz brandy
17 fl oz vegetable stock
2 dessertspoons cornflour
3½ fl oz single cream
½ dessertspoon rosemary
1 dessertspoon thyme
Tamari, (or soy sauce), salt and pepper to taste.

Saute onion, garlic and all herbs.
Add carrot, mushrooms and tamari. Stir continuously until mushrooms release stock.
Add tomato puree, wine, vegetable stock and brandy.
Bring to heat. Make a paste with the cornflour and add to the soup.
Add parsley and cream. (Do not boil after the cream has been added)
Sprinkle on the parsley and a swirl of cream.

Jane Stimpson
Food For Thought
31 Neal Street
Covent Garden
London

Courgette and Rosemary Soup

1 half 1lb courgettes
2 pints chicken stock
2 oz butter
1 half onion

1 small peeled potato
2 tablespoons chopped rosemary
1 half pint double cream

Wash and slice the courgettes, sweat off in a little butter with the sliced onion and the chopped potato, add the rosemary, chicken stock, salt and pepper and poach for 20 minutes. Remove from the stove and blitz in a blender or processor into a smooth puree. Correct seasoning and consistency and serve.

You may accompany this soup with some crispy croutons fried in butter.

Ron Maxfield
Cliveden
Taplow
Berkshire

Petite Soupe de Verdure aux Cuisse de Grenouilles
(Creamed leek and cress soup with frogs' legs)

Yields 1 Litre

300g   fresh frogs' legs
400g   washed and diced leeks
60g   shallots
1 bunch watercress
1 punnet mustard cress
1.5 l chicken fond
60 ml dry white wine
40 ml dry vermouth (Noilly Prat)
90g   butter
100 ml double cream
Little mustard cress for garnish
Salt, pepper, nutmeg.

Firstly trim the frogs' legs removing the feet at the lowest joint. Wash
well. Sweat them in a little butter. Add the white wine and Noilly Prat
and reduce. Pour on the poultry stock. Cover with a lid and simmer gently
until cooked. Remove the frogs' legs and allow to cool. Remove the meat
from the bone as carefully as possible and keep to one side. Place all the
bones back in the stock and allow to simmer for another 15-20 minutes.
Skim and pass through muslin.

Sweat the shallots and leeks under a lid. When soft add the stock. Boil,
skim and simmer until the vegetables are pureed. Wash the mustard cress
and watercress. Blanch in boiling water and drain. Add to the soup, then
pass through a fine sieve or liquidiser. Blend in the cream and remaining
butter. Adjust seasoning.

To serve

Reheat the frogs' legs and divide into individual soup bowls Pour on the
hot soup. Sprinkle with mustard and cress. Serve immediately.

Paul Gayler
Inigo Jones
Garrick Street
London

FISH

Grilled Cod Fillets with Fresh Tomato and Basil Sauce

Make the sauce in advance (it will keep in the refrigerator for two or three days) and you have a quick simple meal. The sauce is long-simmered so that it thickens by reduction. You can easily adjust its consistency to your taste. In the summer, use fresh very ripe tomatoes; otherwise tinned tomatoes are a good substitute. Fresh basil is essential, but if not available try oregano or marjoram instead.
Fillets of hake, haddock or whiting may be substituted for the cod.
This dish is good served with plain potatoes, and frozen petit pois or peas.

Serves 4

4 cod fillets, trimmed
juice of ½ lemon
1-2 tablesp olive oil
freshly ground black pepper
4 basil leaves to garnish

Fresh Tomato and Basil Sauce
1½ lb (750g) very ripe tomatoes, plus 1 tablesp tomato puree (optional)
   or 2 x 14 oz (397g) tins tomatoes
2 spanish onions, finely chopped
3 cloves garlic, finely chopped
4 tablesp olive oil
½ tablesp basil leaves, chopped
1 strip lemon peel
pinch of salt, pinch of sugar, freshly ground black pepper

First make the sauce. If you are using fresh tomatoes, peel and de-seed them. Plunge them into boiling water for a minutes, then, using a fork, lift them out, make a small incision in the skin to peel them. Slice them open and squeeze out the seeds, then coarsely chop the flesh. If the tomatoes are pale and lack flavour, add 1 tablespoon of tomato puree for colour and body.If using tinned tomatoes, de-seed and coarsely chop them, reserving the juice.
Gently soften the chopped onions and garlic in the oil in a heavy pan over gentle heat. Now add the tomatoes, basil, lemon peel and seasoning and simmer for about 20 minutes, stirring occasionally. If you wish for a very smooth sauce, whizz the sauce in a blender or food processor, or rub it through a sieve. The sauce can be gently re-heated when you are ready to serve the fish.
Heat the grill and oil the grill rack. Rinse the fish fillets, pat dry with kitchen paper and brush with a mixture of the lemon juice and 1 or 2 tablespoons of olive oil. Sprinkle with freshly ground black pepper and grill for about 4 minutes, or until the flesh is just opaque.
Pour a puddle of the sauce on to each of four warmed plates and place the fillets on top. Serve straight away, garnished with basil leaves.
To microwave: Prepare as above. Put the fish in a large shallow dish, sprinkle with the lemon juice, cover and cook on High for 8-10 minutes.

Susan Hicks. After the success of her BBC TV series and accompanying book The Fish Course, Susan has now written The Main Course.

Savoury Cod Crumble

This favourite family dish can be cooked in advance and gently re-heated at supper time. It is also ideal for freezing. Serve with a crisp green salad.

Serves 4

1-1½ lb (450-700g) fillets of cod
Semi-skimmed milk for poaching
1-2 tablespoons sunflower oil
4 leeks, trimmed and sliced diagonally, including the tender green parts
4 ribs of celery, scrubbed and finely sliced
6 oz (175g) mushrooms, wiped and quartered
4 hardboiled eggs, peeled and quartered
6 anchovy fillets, each sliced in two lengthways
1 quantity White Sauce, made with poaching milk.
  (See Bechamel sauce recipe)

Crumble topping:
6 oz (175g) wholemeal breadcrumbs
4 oz (100g) Cheddar cheese, grated
2 tablespoon fresh green herbs, (e.g. parsley, coriander, tarragon)
   finely chopped or 2 teaspoons mixed dried herbs
1 oz (25g) butter (optional)

Poach the cod fillets in the milk, remove them from the pan with a slotted spoon and set aside to cool. Reserve the poaching milk for the white sauce. Using a large heavy pan, heat the oil and gently fry the leeks, celery and mushrooms until they are soft but not brown. Allow to cool. Remove any skin and stray bones from the cod fillets, cut into small pieces and gently combine with the vegetables, taking care not to break up the fish or the softened leeks.
Lightly oil a shallow pie or gratin dish, slide in the fish and vegetable mixture, and top with the quarters of hardboiled eggs and anchovy strips. Set the oven to gas mark 5, 375 deg F (190 deg C). Now make the white sauce, using the reserved poaching milk and pour this all over the dish. While the sauce is 'settling' into the dish, prepare the crumble topping by combining the breadcrumbs, grated cheese and herbs and scatter over the top of the pie. Finally, dot with a few scraps of butter if you wish. Bake in the oven for 35 minutes and serve immediately.

Susan Hicks. Susan presented the BBC's, The Fish Course and wrote the accompanying 'The Fish Course' book and now has a new book in print, 'The Main Course'.

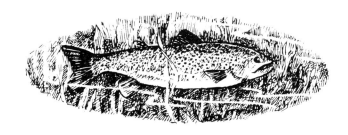

Exotic Fish Pie

Serves 6

If you like fish pie you will welcome any interesting variations. This is far removed from an ordinary nursery fish pie, and is extremely popular in our house, even with the children. Serve it simply with a salad.

1½ lb (675g) potatoes
1¾ lb (800g) skinned cod or whiting fillets
1 larged red pepper
1 large onion
2 oz (50g) butter
3 tablespoons (3 x 15 ml spoon) vegetable oil
1-inch (2.5 cm) piece of fresh ginger
3 cloves of garlic
1 red or green chilli
4 tablespoons (4 x 15 ml spoon) natural yoghurt
2 teaspoons (2 x 5 ml spoon) ground cinnamon
salt

Boil the potatoes and cut into round slices. Cut the fish into 1½ inch (4 cm) chunks. Cut the red pepper and the onion into 1 inch (2.5 cm) pieces.

Melt 1 oz (25g) of the butter and 1 tablespoon (15 ml spoon) of the oil in a large frying pan. Fry the pepper and onion very gently until soft.

Meanwhile peel the ginger and garlic and cut the chilli open under running water, discarding the seeds and stem. Chop the ginger, garlic and chilli together very finely. Remove the pepper and onion from the pan, using a slotted spoon, and put into a large, fairly deep dish in a very cool oven to keep warm.

Add another tablespoon (15 ml spoon) of oil to the pan and heat to medium heat. Put in the fish, chopped ginger, garlic and chilli and cook, turning the pieces gently once or twice, for 5-7 minutes. Sprinkle with salt and add the yoghurt. Allow the yoghurt to become just hot, but not to boil, and then pour the contents of the pan into the serving dish and mix with the pepper and onion.

Finally, heat the remaining 1 oz (25g) butter and tablespoon (15 ml spoon) oil in the pan and add the cinnamon and sliced potatoes. Fry, stirring the potatoes, for about 5 minutes. Top the fish with the fried potatoes and serve.

Josceline Dimbleby, food writer and author of several cookery books, including 'The Josceline Dimbleby Collection' a Sainsbury cookbook.

Glazed Fillet of Turbot with Lemon Thyme Sauce

4 oz turbot fillet per person
topped with scallops mousseline

Scallop Mousse for 4 persons

8 oz scallops
½ pint double cream
salt

Place the scallops into a processor and make them into a puree; pass the puree through a fine sieve and place it in a bowl on ice. When the puree is cool, slowly add the double cream to the mixture then season with salt and a little ground pepper.

Sauce

2 Dover Sole Bones "chopped turbot bones are too strong"

4 sliced shallots   )
4 sliced mushrooms   )   Reduce everything
a sprig of lemon thyme   )
½ bottle dry white wine)   to a glace
½ pint fish stock   )

When the reduction has been done, add 1 pint of double cream. Bring the sauce to the boil, pass it through a fine strainer, correct the seasoning and whisk in 2 oz butter.

Cook the turbot in a little white wine with lemon thyme in the oven so the mousse glazes on top. Remove the turbot when cooked and place onto a warm plate, strain the cooking liquid into the ready prepared sauce, surround the turbot by the sauce and serve with turned new potatoes, samphire and balls of carrots.

Garnish the dish with Lemon Thyme.

Graham Newbould
Inverlochy Castle
Torlundy
Fort William
Scotland

50

A Sandwich of Brill with Salmon and Basil Mousse with a Saffron Sauce and Spaghetti of Carrot

Serves 4 as a main course

1 Brill (6-7 lbs in weight)
7 oz fresh salmon
1 egg white
½ pint double cream
salt, pepper, cayenne
lemon juice
1½ tblsp finely chopped fresh basil
¾ pint fish stock for poaching, made from the bones.

1 large red pepper, skinned, de-seeded and finely diced
3 ripe tomatoes, skinned, de-seeded and finely diced
4 oz Samphire, blanched and refreshed
6-8 long young carrots
4 shallots, finely chopped
1 fl oz white wine vinegar
3 fl oz dry white wine
2 good pinches of saffron threads soaked in a little boiling water
½ clove garlic
1 sprig rosemary
1 tsp crushed white peppercorns
½ pint double cream
salt, cayenne, sugar, lemon juice

Skin and fillet the brill and cut each fillet in two making the tail end
pieces longer than the other. Fold the tail ends underneath to make an
even shape and trim the 8 fillets so that each are roughly the same shape.
Refrigerate.

To make the mousse: Puree the salmon with the egg white in a food
processor and pass through a fine drum sieve into a basin. Set basin over
a larger basin of crushed ice and gradually add the cream, little by
little, mixing in well after each addition until you have a light creamy
mousse that softly holds its shape. Season to taste and stir in the
chopped basil. Refrigerate.

Spaghetti of carrot: Peel the carrots, trim each end and cut, lengthwise,
into long julienne, about ¼ inch square. Cook slowly in a little water
with a knob of butter and a pinch of sugar and salt until the liquid has
evaporated and the 'spaghetti' is very tender.

Spread four of the brill fillets with the salmon mousse about 1 inch thick
and place the remaining fillets on top. Season lightly, butter a saute pan
and place in the stuffed fillets. Pour the cold fish stock around and
cover with a lid. Set aside.

To make the sauce: Sweat the shallots and crushed peppercorns in a small
saucepan with a little butter. Add the wine vinegar, white wine, garlic,
saffron and rosemary and reduce over medium heat until syrupy. Pour in the

double cream and allow to boil gently for a moment. Season to taste with the salt, cayenne, sugar and lemon juice. Set aside.

Over a gentle heat, bring the fish to simmer and cook, covered, very gently for 10-12 minutes. Turn off the heat and leave fish covered for five minutes to finish cooking in its own steam. Remove fish to a plate and cover. Keep warm. Over a medium heat reduce the juices in the pan to two tablespoons. Add the saffron sauce to the pan and stir in. Check seasoning. Keep warm.

Quickly saute the diced pepper in a little olive oil, add the tomato and samphire and remove from heat.
Place the fish on four plates and pour the sauce around through a fine strainer. Scatter the peppers, tomato and samphire over the sauce and place the warm spaghetti of carrot on top of each fish 'sandwich'. Serve.

Mallory Court
Harbury Lane
Tachbrook Mallory
Leamington Spa
Warwickshire

Fillet of Sea Bass baked with Fennel and Fresh Coriander

1 Sea Bass
1 fennel bulb
1 bunch coriander
seasoning
a little butter

To prepare the bass, remove the very sharp fins and descale the fish by scraping with a table knife (I usually do this operation under a tap of running water); gut the fish, clean and fillet, remove all the tiny bones down the middle of the fish, cut into the required number of portions depending on whether it is to be a fish or a main course.

Cut the fennel into ¼ inch sticks and blanch in boiling salted water, scatter on the base of an ovenproof dish with a little fresh coriander; season and brush the flesh side of the fish with melted butter and place on top of the fennel, skin side up. Pour in a little fish stock, brush the skin with melted butter and loosely cover with foil.

Bake until cooked. It is better to undercook slightly as the heat in the fish will continue cooking when the fish has been removed from the oven. For the fish course, serve on small plates with the cooking juices and garnish with fresh coriander or tops of fennel.

Stephen Smith
The Belvedere Hotel
19 North Park Road
Bradford
West Yorkshire

Tronconnettes de Lotte Braisees au Gingembre
et a L'acidule de carotte

Serves 4

Marinade:

3 lb monkfish tail
2 soupspoons ginger trimmings
1 level soup spoon paprika
20 cl olive oil

Skin monkfish and slice into sixteen (16) pieces each about 1 cm thick.
Place the monkfish in a container with the rest of the ingredients.
Marinade for three (3) hours minimum.

Sauce:
4 cl Cognac
4 cl white wine
4 cl veal stock
4 cl fish stock.
2 soupspoons ginger trimmings
2 soupspoons redcurrant jelly
35 cl double cream
salt

Sweat ginger and redcurrant jelly for a minute. Then add the Cognac, the
white wine, the veal stock and the fish stock. Reduce to a syrup. Add the
cream and boil for 5 minutes, salt to taste.

Julienne:
3 medium carrots cut in julienne
1 soupspoon ginger cut in julienne
1 soupspoon redcurrant jelly
30 g butter
salt

Sweat the julienne of ginger in the butter with the redcurrant jelly. Add
the julienne of carrot and sweat together. Season to taste and cook until
al dente (approximately 3-4 minutes).

Cooking:
1 tefal pan
20 cl fish stock
salt

Using a dry tefal pan, give the fish a light colouring on both sides.
Deglaze with fish stock. Remove fish when cooked. Reduce your stock and
then add your sauce. Reduce further until you reach a coating consistancy.
Pass your sauce through a sieve. Season to taste.

Garnish:
Chervil leaves
1 to 2 courgettes

Cut and prepare your courgettes into sixteen (16) fans. Arrange for (4) pieces of monkfish per plate and the julienne in the middle. Garnish alternately with courgette fans. Pour the sauce. Finish with chervil leaves.

Michel Perraud
Les Alouettes
High Street
Claygate
Surrey

Terrine of Smoked Fish in Smoked Salmon Jelly with Vouvray Mayonnaise

Smoked halibut
Smoked eel
Smoked trout
Smoked salmon
Tomato petals
Basil
Chervil
Smoked salmon consomme, jellied
Mayonnaise flavoured with mustard and Vouvray

Line an oblong terrine with sliced halibut.

Pour a little smoked salmon consomme on top of the halibut and allow to set.

Layer eel in the terrine then a layer of trout, then basil, then tomato petals then basil, salmon and chervil.

Add smoked salmon jelly in between each of the above layers.

Once you have completed the above repeat the layering process, but in the opposite order to above, and again set in smoked salmon consomme.

Once you have completed the layering then seal in the top layer with a covering of smoked halibut.

Place in the fridge, and allow to set overnight.

Cut into slices and serve on a Vouvray mayonnaise.

Keith Stanley
Head Chef
The Ritz
Piccadilly
London

Fillet of Red Mullet baked with Braised Onion, Tomato and Thyme and served on a Rosti Potato with a Cream Sauce

Serves 4

2 x 1 lb Red Mullet
2 large new potatoes
4 large onions
2 tomatoes
1 sprig of fresh thyme
6 fl oz dry white wine
½ pint fish stock
½ pint double cream
2 oz unsalted butter

Scale and fillet the mullet, leaving the skin on, and place in the fridge.

Peel and finely slice the onions. Put a thick bottomed pan on a high heat and add just enough vegetable oil to cover the bottom of the pan. Add the onions and stir. Reduce the heat to moderate and place a close-fitting lid on the pan and leave to stew for about 5-10 minutes. Take off the lid and the onions should have started to caramalize. Add a little cold water and mix into the onions taking up any sediment in the pan. Repeat this action until the onions are soft and brown and most of the liquid has evaporated. Add salt and mill pepper to taste. Remove from the heat and keep to one side.

Blanch, refresh and peel the tomatoes. Scoop out the seeds and neatly dice the flesh. Pick off the leaves of thyme and add to the diced tomato. Put to one side.

Boil the fish stock down gently until it has reduced by ¾. Add 3 fl oz of white wine and reduce further by ¾. Add the ½ pint of double cream and gently reduce again by ¾. Take off the heat and whisk in the 2 oz of butter until emulsified. Season with a little salt and ground white pepper. Keep warm.

Peel and grate the potato on a cheese grater and dry in a clean tea towel. Place a small thick bottomed frying pan over a moderate heat and add enough vegetable oil to coat the bottom of the pan. Put in the potato and spread so there is enough to cover the bottom of the pan. Gently fry until golden brown on each side. Repeat so you have four potatoes. Keep warm.

Place the braised onion into a thick bottomed shallow sided pan in four equal portions. Place the fish on top and sprinkle with the tomato and thyme mixture. Season with salt and pepper and add the remaining white wine to the pan (there should be enough liquid to cover the bottom). Cover with kitchen foil and place in a pre-heated oven at gas mark 7 for about 10-12 minutes. Take out when cooked and keep warm.

To serve: Place the warmed potato on the middle of a warmed plate. Using a fish slice, scoop up the fish and onions and put on top of the potato. Pour the sauce around the fish and serve immediately.

Chef's Notes:

Fish stock can be replaced by adding 4 fl oz of dry vermouth to the white wine when making the sauce but increase the butter by a further 2 oz to mellow the sauce. Ask your fishmonger to prepare the fish and to take out the small bones in the fillets.

Chris Oakes
Oakes Restaurant
169 Slad Road
Stroud
Gloucestershire

Fish Terrine with Herb Sauce

2 large lemon soles
1 lb whiting
3 egg whites
3 slices bread soaked in milk
7 oz double cream
1 soupspoon tomato puree
1 teaspoon nutmeg
1 soupspoon chopped chives
1 teaspoon chopped dill
7 oz chopped onions
7 oz sliced mushrooms
2 oz butter
4 large pancakes
salt and pepper

Skin and fillet the soles and whiting. Cook the onion and mushroom gently in the butter. Blend the whiting to a puree in a food processor and season with salt, pepper, nutmeg, chives, dill and tomato puree. Add the squeezed out bread and blend well. Blend in the egg whites and chill for an hour. Add the cold cream and blend. Oil a rectangular terrine and line it with the pancakes. Mix a quarter of the fish puree with the mushroom mixture. Spread half of the remaining puree over the base of the terrine and cover with the seasoned sole fillets. Next spread a layer of the fish/mushroom mixture and cover with the remainder of the fillets. Finish with a layer of the fish puree. Fold over the flaps of pancake to cover, lay a sheet of foil on top and bake in a moderate oven, in a bain marie, for about 1½ hours. Serve with a homemade mayonnaise into which a little sorrel and lemon juice has been blended.

The Kings Arms Restaurant
Old Amersham
Buckinghamshire

56

Galantine of Chew Valley Lake or Pink Trout with Grape Sauce

Serves 6

butter
1 oz (25g) onion, diced
7 trout fillets, skinned, approximately 3 oz each,
    plus 4 oz. (125g) extra, also skinned
1 oz (25g) fresh white bread (thin, no crust)
½ small egg white
1-2 tablespoons single cream
salt and freshly-ground black pepper
freshly-grated nutmeg
dash of English mustard powder
4 fl oz (125ml) double cream, whipped
1 heaped teaspoon fresh dill, chopped
fish stock

Melt 1 tablespoon of butter, add the onion and cook without colouring, then leave to cool. Place the 4 oz (125g) trout fillets on a dish with the onion and bread. Moisten the fish with the egg white, add the single cream and sprinkle on salt, freshly-ground black pepper, nutmeg and a dash of mustard powder. Cover and chill.

Place the ingredients in a food processor, mix well and pass through a sieve. Place in a bowl, on ice, and gradually beat in the whipped cream and dill.

Place the remaining trout fillets between two sheets of polythene and lightly flatten them with a cutlet bat or rolling pin. Season the fillets with salt, pepper, nutmeg and a little mustard powder and lay flat on a large sheet of buttered foil, ensuring that all the fillets are side by side with the edges slightly overlapping. Fill any gaps with odd trimmings of the fillets. Pipe the trout forcemeat on to the fillets, covering them completely. Roll the mixture up as you would a Swiss roll, using the foil and twisting at each end. Chill for 2-3 hours, then unwrap gently and re-roll the sausage, this time using a clean, old tea-towel. Tie the ends securely. Place the whole thing in a pot or deep-sided tray of fish stock to cover and simmer for 30 minutes. Cool in the stock and when cold, chill in the refrigerator.

For the Grape Sauce

juice of 3 lemons or limes
2 tablespoons caster sugar
5 tablespoons gin
1½ lbs. (700g) grapes, skinned
1 tablespoon arrowroot

To make the sauce, place the lemon or lime juice, sugar and gin in a pan and reduce. Add the grapes and cook for 2 minutes so that the grapes are just lightly cooked. Removed the grapes and place in a clean bowl. Add arrowroot to the liquor just to thicken. Sieve the juice over the grapes and leave to cool.

Remove the galantine from the refrigerator and unwrap. Cut into thin slices and arrange on a plate with a garnish of assorted lettuces tossed in vinaigrette, lemon wedges and the grape sauce.

Robert Elsmore
Hunstrete House
Hunstrete
Chelwood
Near Bristol
Avon

Salmon Kedgeree

12 oz long grain rice
4 oz butter
½ teaspoon cayenne pepper
pinch of saffron or turmeric
mace
1 large or 2 small onions
8 oz fresh salmon
4 eggs
1 dessertspoon chopped parsley

Cook rice in the normal manner, refresh till cool and put aside. Meanwhile, hard boil the eggs, cool, peel and put aside.

Finely chop the onion and sweat in a large pan (Skillet), over medium heat, with half the butter, add the cayenne pepper, blade of mace and salmon. Stir for about 4 minutes, till salmon is cooked then add the rice, chopped eggs, parsley and remaining butter, stir for 3-4 minutes, till hot all through.

Serve immediately.

*Turmeric can be used here but it will only give the colour and not the flavour of Saffron.

Stephen and Anne Frost
The Stonor Arms
Stonor
Nr Henley-on-Thames
Oxfordshire

Monkfish with Mustard and Cucumber Sauce

1 Monktail
1 tablespoon Dijon mustard
¼ pint fish stock - 1 medium sized leek
                    1 medium sized shallot
                    1 small bunch parsley
2 fluid oz double cream
1 oz unsalted butter
1 fluid oz dry sherry
1 cucumber - peeled
½ lemon
Olive oil for frying

With a small sharp knife cut away the two fillets from the one central
bone. Try to keep the knife pointed slightly inwards towards the bone so
that if your hand slips you are cutting against the bone rather than
damaging the fish fillet.

Cut away the two "cheeks" which are attached to the fillets, then carefully
trim off the membrane and any discoloured patches.

If you are not going to use the fish immediately put it in a refrigerator
either wrapped in clingfilm if it is to be used within a few hours or else
lightly brushed with olive oil. Remember not to put the fish next to the
eggs, milk or anything else likely to taint.

Just before you complete the dish, slice the fish into medallions no more
than a ¼ inch thick.

To prepare the fish stock

Cut the bone and all the fish trimmimngs into roughly 1 inch pieces. Clean
and cut the leek, shallot and parsley similarly. Grind a little black
pepper over the pieces.

Warm a teaspoonful of olive oil in a medium (say 2 pint) saucepan. Then
sweat the fish and vegetables until you can smell cooked fish rather than
raw.

Add all the peelings from the cucumber and 1 pint of water. Bring this to
the boil then turn down the heat and simmer for 20 minutes.

Strain into a smaller saucepan and reduce by simmering until you have ¼
pint left.

To make the sauce

Cut the cucumber, as you prefer, either into thin slices or thin strips.
Lightly salt and pepper them. Keep them to one side in a warm spot in the
kitchen.

Whisk the tablespoon of mustard into the fish stock and sherry and bring to the boil.

Add the cream. Reboil and then simmer for 5 minutes. Whisk in the butter. Take the sauce off the heat.

To complete the dish

Heat a dry pan until you sense it is about to start smoking.

Place the thin slices of monk onto the hot surface of the pan and let them seal of each side. Dust with a fine spray of salt. They will cook in two or three minutes.

Lift the slices of monkfish onto a piece of kitchen paper and squeeze lemon over them.

Test the sauce to see whether it may need a little salt. Spoon the sauce onto warm plates.

Lift the cucumber which will have shed some of its juices. Squeeze it lightly and place onto the sauce.

Lay the monkfish on top.

Shaun Hill
Gidleigh Park
Chagford
Devon

Sliced Salmon with a Tomato and Basil Vinaigrette

5 oz Salmon, thinly sliced (as in smoked salmon)

Vinaigrette

5 fl oz sherry vinegar
1 tblsp olive oil
2 pinches salt
2 tomatoes (blanched, de-seeded and chopped roughly)
3 or 4 basil leaves (roughly chopped)

Mix vinegar, olive oil, salt and pepper together and whisk. Add tomatoes and basil, stir in and keep at room temperature. Cook salmon under fierce heat for 10-15 seconds, place on plate and keep warm. Spoon over vinaigrette and serve with basil leaves and lemon.

James Macbeth
Skippers Bistro
1A Dock Place
Leith
Edinburgh

Skewered Scallops and Oysters wrapped in smoked Bacon and Served with Sweet Peppers

Serves 4

8 scallops and corals
12 oysters
14 thin rashers of smoked back bacon
2 red peppers
1 yellow pepper
1 green pepper
2 blanched tomatoes
12 cloves garlic (blanched 3 times)
14 small blanched shallots
Few sprigs of thyme
2 onions, thinly sliced
Olive oil
½ glass white wine
Butter

4 wooden skewers

Roll the oysters in the bacon and place one onto a skewer. Follow this by adding one roe, one scallop and repeat this for the rest of the skewer - three oysters, two scallops and two roes in each skewer.

Cut peppers into ½ inch strips and then cut a few strips diagonally into diamonds - to provide five diamonds of each colour. Chop remaining peppers and 2 shallots into small pieces, place in a pan with a little white wine and cook until tender. Pass through a sieve and season.

Cut the remaining two rashers of bacon into thin strips and fry in their own fat until crispy. Saute the garlic cloves and remaining shallots in bacon fat and olive oil until golden.

Cut the blanched tomato into neat diamonds the same size as the peppers. Cook the onions and pepper diamonds in some olive oil with the thyme. When soft add the bacon and tomatoes.

Warm the pepper sauce. Cook the kebab by either frying or grilling on a hot grill plate which will take only a few minutes.

Place the onion and pepper mix around the plate. Pour the sauce in the centre and garnish with shallots and garlic. Lay the kebab in the centre and serve.

Gary Rhodes
The Castle at Taunton
Castle Green
Taunton
Somerset

61

Roulade de sole et Saumon au Mirepoix

(Fillet of Salmon and Sole steamed on a Brunoise of Vegetables)

Serves 4

4 x 100g fillets of Sole
4 x 60g Salmon fillets
salt and freshly ground pepper
nutmeg
60g leaf spinach
75g Brunoise of vegetables
5 cl vermouth
10 cl white wine
20 cl sauce Jacqueline
60 g butter
12 baby carrots
60 g butter to finish
picked chervil

Trim and batton the salmon and sole fillets and season with salt and
freshly ground pepper.
Place the spinach upon the sole fillet and salmon upon the spinach and roll
into a ballontine.
Wrap in a little cling wrap and tie both the ends.
Steam the packet in a vapeur until cooked. Remove, dry and keep warm.
Place the vegetables in a little butter and saute with no colour.
Deglace with the vermouth and white wine and reduce by one half.
Remove the vegetables not allowing them to discolour or overcook.
Add the sauce jacqueline and reduce to the correct consistency.
Mount with butter and add the vegetables back to the sauce.
Check the seasoning and place upon the serving plate.
Slice the roulade into four even pieces and place upon the sauce.
Re-heat the baby carrots and place between the fish. Garnish with picked
chervil.
Serve immediately.

Colin John Bussey
The Gleneagles Hotel
Auchterarder
Perthshire
Scotland

Pan Fried Salmon with a Red Wine Sauce and a garnish of Roast Artichokes, Potatoes and Baby Onions

Serves 8

2½ lb (1.1 kg) Salmon, filleted and scaled with the skin
        remaining*
12oz (350g) potatoes, peeled
1 lb (450g) Jerusalem Artichokes, peeled
8 oz (225g) Baby Onions, peeled
1½ pints (900 ml) Red Beaujolais wine
6 oz (175g) shallots
4 oz (100g) button mushrooms, sliced
sprig of thyme
1 oz (25g) parsley
Salmon head or Salmon bones
2 pints (1.1 litres) water
¾ pint (450 ml) veal stock or beef stock
vegetable oil
salt and pepper
½ oz (15g) sugar
4 oz (100g) butter

*If you wish to simplify the proccess, the skin can be removed completely.

The Fish Stock:

In 1 oz (25g) butter "sweat" 4 oz (100g) shallots, the mushrooms, thyme, parsley stalks and salmon head/bones. After approximately 5 minutes add 1 pint (600 ml) red wine, bring to the boil and reduce by half. Add sufficient cold water to cover, bring to the boil again, then simmer for 30 minutes, skimming regularly. Remove from heat and leave to settle then pass through a fine sieve.

The Garnish:

Using a No. 25/2 cm diameter parisienne cutter (melon baller) scoop the artichokes and potatoes into neat round shapes, and roast in the oven until golden brown in 1 oz (25g) butter and 4 tablespoons of oil. Meanwhile, place the onions in a pan together with a little water, salt and pepper, sugar and the remaining 2 oz (50g) butter, and simmer until just cooked. Place on one side.

The Sauce:

Finely chop the remaining 2 oz (50g) shallots and "sweat" in 1 tablespoon of oil. Add ½ pint (300ml) red wine and reduce to a glaze. Add the fish stock and veal stock to the pan and reduce liquid by approximately three quarters, skimming regularly. When ready, pass through a fine sieve and keep warm.

The Salmon:

Cut the salmon into ¼ inch thick slices and fry in a little oil over a high heat for approximately 10-15 seconds each side; this leaves the fish moist in the middle.

To Finish:

Arrange a combination of the re-heated artichokes, potatoes and baby onions in a 'pile' at the top of the plate. Set out the slices of salmon (4 or 5 per person) in a semi-circle. Surround with the sauce and serve immediately.

David Watson
Pool Court Restaurant
Pool-in-Wharfedale
Otley
West Yorkshire

Roast Monkfish Tails with Light Sherry Sauce

6-7oz monkfish tail (fillet by taking knife down either end
                    of centre bone, use bones for stock)
Fish Stock

lemon, parsley (any other herbs such as basil tarragon etc) and bones, cook stock for 17 minutes and strain.

Sauce

Double or whipping cream
salt and pepper
2 tblsp dry sherry
1 egg yolk

Place the monkfish in seasoned flour and then on to a greased (olive oil) tray. Roast in a high heat in oven until crisp and golden brown.

Sauce: Reduce stock by half, add sherry and double or whipping cream, salt and pepper to taste and yolk of one egg. Cook over reduced heat until slightly thickened then cover plate with a thin layer of sauce and place monkfish on top. Serve immediately.

James Macbeth
Skippers Bistro
1A Dock Place
Leith
Edinburgh

A Fricassee of Turbot and Vegetables

Fingers of turbot cooked in a champagne sauce with salmon caviar and noodles.

Serves 1

8 fingers of turbot cut diagonally from the fillet 2½ x ½ x ½ inches.
2 of each turned; mushrooms, carrots, swede, broccoli, onions (lightly cooked in a steamer.
a small amount of salmon caviar.
3 oz champagne sauce.
3 oz green noodles.
sprig of flat parsley
½ oz finely chopped shallots.
butter.

Fry shallots in butter without colouring.
Add sauce and heat to near boiling point. Just before serving drop in finger of turbot and stand on the side of stove until just cooked, add salmon caviar and serve. DO NOT OVERCOOK.
Place noodles in the centre of plate carefully arrange the turbot around the noodles and dress vegetables on the turbot.
Dress noodles with a little more caviar and parsley.

A Champagne Sauce

Makes 1 pint.

½ pint cream, whipped
1 oz chopped onion
½ pint fish stock
½ pint champagne
4-6 oz softened butter
seasoning and lemon juice

Reduce onion, fish stock and champagne by half, add cream. Strain, season add lemon to taste, remove from heat whisk in butter. DO NOT BOIL AFTER ADDING BUTTER TO THE SAUCE.

Homemade Spinach Noodles

serves 8

1 lb strong flour
3 eggs
1 soup spoon olive oil
seasoning
4 oz cooked baby spinach (dry and finely chopped)

In processor add all ingredients and mix to a very firm paste.
Rest for 5 minutes.
Roll out using pasta machine, numbers 1.3.5.7. Dry for 5 minutes before

cutting, use thin cutter.
Boil in plenty of water with a little oil and seasoning for 3 minutes,
refresh in cold water, strain and toss in a little walnut oil, reheat in
steamer.

DO MAKE SURE THE PASTE IS DRY. DO NOT OVERCOOK THE NOODLES. USE LESS EGGS
IF SPINACH IS WET AND FINELY CHOPPED.

Nick Buckingham
Cavendish Hotel
Baslow
Derbyshire

Delice de Barbue au Fenouil

Steamed Brill with fennel and pernod sauce.

Serves 4

4 x 160g brill fillets
salt and freshly ground pepper
30g butter
30g shallots
10cl Pernod
5cl white wine
20cl fish stock
20cl double cream
100g fennel
30g chopped dill
60g blanched tomato pieces
60g butter to finish
picked dill

Season and steam the brill fillets to taste, remove dry and keep warm.
Place some butter into a saucepan and place the shallots in and cook with
no colour.
Deglace with the pernod and add the white wine and reduce by one half.
Pour in the fish stock and further reduce by two thirds to a glace stage.
Add the double cream and pass through a fine sieve and return to the stove.
Saute the fennel in a little butter and roll in the chopped dill once again
remove, dry and keep warm.
Reheat the blanched tomato pieces and evenly place upon the top of the
fish.
Mount the butter into the sauce and place upon the serving plate.
Garnish with the fennel and place the fish upon the top.
Place the picked dill upon the top and serve immediately.

Alan J Hill
The Gleneagles Hotel
Auchterarder
Perthshire
Scotland

Sea Bass in Pastry with Sorrel and Mushrooms

The sea bass is a summer fish - the first few are brought into the restaurant in April and May, but by July and August they are in full flood, some small enough to serve whole for one diner alone, and others reaching as much as 8 lb. or so in weight.
It is one of the finest of fish, with its firm sweet flesh. Recently it has become very fashionable in many a restaurant, but we have always thought of it as very much a local catch - a fish that amateur fishermen might catch on holiday in Dartmouth, sometimes bringing it back to sell to us.

Serves 4

2 oz sorrel
1 shallot, chopped
1 oz butter
4 oz mushrooms, chopped
salt and pepper
1½ lb sea bass, skinned and filleted
8 oz shortcrust pastry
1 egg, beaten

Sauce
1 shallot, chopped
2 fl oz fish stock
2 oz white wine
1 egg
2 oz sorrel
salt and pepper
3 oz butter, melted and cooled until just warm

Cut any tough stalks from the sorrel and discard. Shred finely. Sweat the shallot in the butter until beginning to soften, then add the mushrooms, salt and pepper. Cook until tender, then turn up heat, and bubble until mushroom liquid is almost entirely evaporated. Add the sorrel, and stir for a few seconds. Remove from the heat. Taste and adjust seasonings, then leave to cool.

Season the fillets of fish, then sandwich with half the stuffing. Spread the remainder on the top. Roll out the pastry thinly, and wrap around the bass, enclosing completely. Tuck the joints underneath. Lift onto a metal baking sheet and rest in a cool place for half an hour. Brush with egg, and bake for 20 minutes at 230C/450F/Gas mark 8 until nicely browned

To make the sauce put the shallot in a small pan with the fish stock and white wine. Boil until almost dry. Spoon into a blender with the egg, sorrel, salt and pepper. Set the blender going and trickle in the melted butter a very little at a time to make an emulsion. To keep warm, pour the sauce into a bowl, over a pan of almost simmering water making sure that the base of the bowl is not immersed.

Serve the sauce with the Sea Bass in Pastry.

Joyce Molyneux
The Carved Angel
2 South Embankment
Dartmouth
South Devon

Oban Bay Scallops in Cream Cheese Sauce with Strips of Vegetables

16 pieces of fresh cleaned scallops cut in half
4 sprigs of dill
½ pint of double cream
1 measure of white wine
½ finely chopped onion
2 oz cream cheese
1 small piece of carrot, leek, courgette and turnip cut into
  matchstick shapes
salt and pepper
1 oz unsalted butter
1 teaspoon of whipped double cream
2 egg yolks
8 leaves of cut cleaned spinach

Melt half the butter in a thick bottomed pan, add scallops and strips of vegetables. Cook lightly without colouring the scallops. Add white wine to pan and bring to boil. Remove scallops and vegetables and put to one side. Reduce cooking wine by 2/3rds. Add pouring cream and season. When sauce has reached consistency to coat the back of a wooden spoon, remove from heat and add the scallops and vegetables to the sauce. Cook off spinach and onions in a little butter and place pile of spinach on each plate. Put sauce back on gas and add cream cheese then add more seasoning if needed. Remove sauce from gas, add whipped cream and egg yolks slowly stirring. Place scallops and sauce onto spinach. Place each plate under grill and glaze, garnish plates with one sprig of fresh dill. Serve.

Brian Graham
Shieldhill
Quothquan
Biggar
Lanarkshire
Scotland

Fish Cakes

Good fish cakes are universally popular (especially with children). The time-honoured combination of fish and potatoes can be the basis for an infinite combination of ingredients. Home-made fish cakes are also much better than the frozen or shop-bought variety. Perhaps the most popular are the simplest; a mixture of plain mashed potatoes, coarsely chopped parsley and really fresh cooked white fish such as cod, haddock or whiting. Shaped into cakes or croquettes, and rolled in lightly seasoned flour, dipped in beaten egg and breadcrumbs, or coated with sesame seeds or oatmeal, they should be shallow fried or baked in the oven and served immediately - with tomato sauce, tartare sauce, mayonnaise or just a squeeze of citrus juice (lemon, lime or orange). Use a good tasty variety of potato and do not be tempted to add too much butter, cream or milk when you mash them, or soggy fish cakes will result. Here is a basic recipe and some useful variations.

Favourite Fish Cakes

Although these are best made with freshly cooked fish, they are still very good if left-over cooked fish is used. A green salad is an excellent accompaniment.

Makes 8 to 10 fish cakes.

1-1½ lb (500-750g) white fish fillets, (cod, haddock, ling, whiting,
    pollack, coley etc.) skinned
1½ lb (750g) potatoes
1-2 oz (25-50g) butter
pinch of salt, freshly ground black pepper
2 good tablespoons parsley, coarsely chopped
1 teaspoon cayenne pepper (optional)
1 egg
4 oz (125g) breadcrumbs
sunflower oil for frying
fresh tomato sauce to tomato ketchup to serve

Scrub the potatoes (do not peel), cut into even-sized chunks and cook in a large covered pan of boiling salted water until just soft.
Heat the grill and oil the grill rack. Dot the fish fillets with a few scraps of butter, season lightly with salt and black pepper and grill them for 2 to 4 minutes, according to their thickness. Let them cool, then flake them and remove any stray bones.
Drain the cooked potatoes, peel off their skins and mash them with the butter if you wish. Beat with a wooden spoon for a smooth texture. Fork in the parsley, then the flakes of cooked fish and check the seasoning, adding cayenne pepper if you wish. Chill the mixture for a few hours, or overnight.
When you are ready to cook, beat the egg, and place the breadcrumbs on a dinner plate. Shape a handful of the fish mixture into a ball in your hands, then flatten it into a cake. Dip it in the egg, then turn it on the plate of breadcrumbs so that it is well coated. You should get 8 to 10 fish cakes from this quantity of mixture.
When you are ready to eat, heat up a little oil in a heavy frying pan and

fry the fish cakes for 2 or 3 minutes on each side until they are crisp and hot right through. Serve straight away with Fresh Tomato Sauce or tomato ketchup. Variations on this basic recipe follow.

Fresh Tomato Sauce
Makes 10 fl oz (300ml)

1-1½ lb (500-750g) ripe, juicy tomatoes, peeled and deseeded
1 tablespoon olive oil
½ tablespoon finely chopped fresh herbs
1-2 teaspoons tomato puree
freshly ground black pepper

Place all the ingredients in a large heavy pan and simmer for 15 minutes, stirring occasionally, until the sauce is reduced. If the colour is pale, add a little more tomato puree. Serve the sauce hot or cold. You can process it in a food processor or blender if you want a smoother texture.

Smoked Salmon Fish Cakes with Dill and Soured Cream Dressing

Using the same basic ingredients as for Favourite Fish Cakes, add 2-3 oz (50-75g) finely chopped smoked salmon (you can buy cheap offcuts from your fishmonger) and substitute finely chopped fresh dill for the parsley. When serving, pour a spoonful of soured cream over each fish cake and garnish with a sprig of dill.

Lemony Fish Croquettes with Hazelnut Coating

Add the very finely grated rind of 1 lemon to the basic Favourite Fish Cakes mixture, sprinkle with a little lemon juice and substitute 1 tablespoon finely chopped coriander leaves for the 2 tablespoons chopped parsley. Grind 4 oz (125g) hazelnuts in a food processor or coffee grinder fairly finely. Shape the chilled mixture into croquettes, brush with beaten egg, coat with hazelnuts and shallow fry in sunflower oil, turning all the time for even cooking. Serve on nests of salad leaves with a yoghurt and mayonnaise dressing.

Boursin Fish Cakes with Sesame Seed Coating

These fish cakes have a wonderful crisp crunchy coating and a melting creamy centre. Use the same basic ingredients as for Favourite Fish Cakes. When you are rolling a ball of the mixture in your hands, push a teaspoon of Boursin or a similar garlic-and-herb flavoured soft cheese into the centre of the ball. Alternatively, mix a crushed clove of garlic into a teaspoon of plain soft cheese and push it into the centre of the ball. Shape the mixture all around the cheese, then flatten it into a fish cake, dip in beaten egg and coat well with sesame seeds. Shallow-fry in the usual way.

Father's Fish Cakes

My father was the fish expert in our home. He remembers that when he was a child in Yorkshire, his local fish shop sold the most marvellous little fish cakes for a halfpenny (½d) for two (fine fast food!) - and these you ate from your hand as you walked home from school.

12 oz (350g) white fish fillets, (for instance, cod, hake, brill or
    whiting), skinned
6 large potatoes
pinch of salt, freshly ground black pepper
sunflower oil for deep-frying
1 quantity Batter No 2 or 3 (see below)

First scrub the potatoes and cook in a covered pan of boiling salted water until they are half-cooked. You can peel them before or after cooking, as you prefer. Allow to cool enough to handle and slice into ¼ inch (0.5cm) rounds.
Check that no bones remain in the fish fillets, wash them, and pat dry with kitchen paper. Mince with fish by chopping thoroughly on a board with a very sharp knife. Season with salt and pepper.
When you are ready to cook, heat the oil in a wok or deep-fryer. Sandwich 1-2 tablespoons minced fish between 2 slices of potato, and carry on in this way until you have used all the fish and potatoes. Coat each fish cake in batter, drop into the hot oil and cook for 2 or 3 minutes or until golden brown. Serve straight away.

Batters

1. Tempura batter
This very light batter gives a crisp snowy appearance and is suitable for coating deep-fried small pieces of fish and shellfish. It does not need 'resting' time and should be made just before it is needed.
1 egg
8 fl oz (250ml) iced water
4 oz (125g) white flour, sifted

Using a balloon whisk or fork, lightly mix together all the ingredients until smooth. Do not beat or overmix. Use straight away.

2. Simple Blender batter
You may adjust the amount of milk used in this traditional batter, depending on whether you need a thin or slightly thicker mixture.
4 oz (125g) plain flour, sifted
1 egg
pinch of salt
5-6 tablespoons skimmed milk

Put all the ingredients into the bowl of a food processor or blender and whizz for about 45 seconds or until the mixture is smooth. Leave the batter to rest for an hour before using.

3. Beer batter
4 oz (125g) plain flour, sifted
3 tablespoons olive oil
about 8 fl oz (250ml) beer or water
1-2 egg whites

Put the flour into a mixing bowl and make a well in the centre. Pour in the oil and, using a balloon whisk or wooden spoon, beat it thoroughly into the flour. Add the beer gradually, beating from the outside of the bowl towards the centre. Set aside until you are ready to cook, then whisk the egg whites fairly stiffly and fold them into the batter. Use straight away.

Susan Hicks. After the success of her BBC TV series and accompanying book The Fish Course, Susan has now written The Main Course.

Deep Ocean Terrine

Serves 12

120g sliced Halibut
120g sliced Monkfish
120g sliced Coley
120g sliced Gurnet
300g sliced Salmon
2 medium sized leeks
Smoked Salmon
Cayenne Pepper
Sea salt
Dill for garnish

Lemon Butter
50g shallots finely chopped
chopped dill
zest of 1 lemon
juice of 1 lemon and lemon segments
250g of unslated butter
Pestel and Mortar and seasoning

Slice all fish as for smoked salmon. Season on a buttered tray and sprinkle with cayenne pepper and grill very lightly till just cooked. Sweat off sliced leeks, season and drain. Line terrine with smoked salmon. Whilst still warm layer in the fish, white fish then salmon, repeat, then place leeks in middle. When full press for 1 hour refrigerate. Serve with lemon butter (or a lemon butter sauce) and small salad.

Nigel Haworth
Northcote Manor
Northcote Road
Langho
Blackburn
Lancashire

Bouillabaisse

This classic dish, for which there are countless different recipes, offers great scope to the adventurous fish cook. It is a one-pot soup or stew, originating in the French Mediterranean where many otherwise ignored species of fish are used with flair and imagination. The sequence of cooking should be carefully timed and planned so that all the prepared ingredients are cooked to perfection. To give flavour, use inexpensive fish like fillets of coley or whiting which will disintegrate and add body to the soup. Add small whole gurnard or red mullet for their flamboyant appearance, and finer firm-fleshed fish like monkfish, bass or John Dory. Shellfish can be added too. To serve, the fish is lifted from the stew and put into shallow soup bowls and the soup or broth is poured around it. The essential saffron, olive oil and rouille provide the classic basis of the dish, but the taste and appearance of every bouillabaisse depends upon the choice of available fish. You will need a very large heavy saucepan for this dish.

Serves 8 - 10

2½ lb (1.25kg) assorted fish (e.g. cod, haddock, hake, ling, catfish,
   dogfish or whiting; then gurnard, redfish or red mullet; and
   John Dory, bass or monkfish)
8 oz (250g) shellfish (Dublin Bay prawns, whole shrimps or mussels)
3-4 tablespoons olive oil
3 fat cloves garlic, crushed
2 large onions, chopped
2 sticks celery, roughly chopped
1 lb (500g) tomatoes, peeled and coarsely chopped
Bouquet garni
2 pieces orange peel
4 pints (2.3 litres) boiling water
pinch of salt, freshly ground black pepper
1 sachet saffron powder
2 potatoes, peeled and sliced
1-2 tablespoons chopped parsley to garnish
1 quantity Rouille (see below) and French or garlic bread to serve

First clean and prepare the fish. Cut the larger fish like cod or John Dory into steaks, cutlets or fillets; gut, scale if necessary and leave whole the small gurnards, red mullet or redfish; wash all the fish and pat dry. Rinse the prawns or shrimps, scrub the mussels if using, and set aside.
Heat the oil in a large heavy saucepan and gently fry the garlic, onions and celery until pale and soft. Add the tomatoes, bouquet garni and orange peel, pour in the boiling water, bring back to the boil and stir whilst boiling hard for 3 or 4 minutes until the resulting basic soup has slightly thickened.
Now turn down the heat and add the softer fillets of inexpensive fish, like coley, whiting or dogfish. Add a pinch of salt, a good shake of pepper and the saffron powder. Top with the potato slices and simmer for 10 to 15 minutes. Now add the small whole fish, and the pieces of cod, hake, monkfish or John Dory. Continue to simmer for a further 10 minutes, then add the mussels, prawns or shrimps and cook for a further 5 minutes or

until the fish is cooked and the mussels (if using) have opened.
Using a perforated spoon, transfer the fish, shellfish and potatoes to a
large warmed serving dish, or divide among eight to ten shallow soup bowls.
Strain the remaining soup through a colander or sieve and pour it over and
around the fish. Sprinkle with chopped parsley and serve straight away
with the Rouille and warmed French or garlic bread. Provide knives, forks
and soup spoons, and a dish for discarded mussel shells and fish bones.

Rouille

This fiery sauce is not a mayonnaise, but the method of making it is rather
similar. It gives an authentic touch to Bouillabaisse and other
Mediterranean fish stews or soups.

Makes about 5 fl oz (150ml)

2-3 fat cloves garlic, chopped
1 slice white bread, crust removed
a little fish stock or water
2 red chilli peppers, finely chopped
3 tablespoons good quality olive oil

Pound the garlic to a paste with a pestle and mortar (or use the end of a
wooden rolling pin or the back of a wooden spoon in a sturdy bowl).
Squeeze out the slice of bread in a little fish stock or water and pound
this and the chilli peppers into the garlic paste. Now add the olive oil
drop by drop, beating all the time, until you have a smooth and creamy red
sauce.

Susan Hicks. Susan's latest book The Main Course follows on from the
success of her BBC TV series and accompanying book, The Fish Course.

74

Fillet of Sole with Mushrooms and Capers

½ lb fillet of Lemon Sole
¼ lb button mushrooms
2 oz chopped capers
1 small onion, very finely chopped
breadcrumbs mix - breadcrumbs (fresh)
                    1 oz mozzarello
                    1 oz cheddar
                    1 oz parmesan - all grated and mixed with
                                breadcrumbs

Poach sole (or bake in oven) for 1 minute. Gently fry onions and mushrooms
and capers. Meanwhile take sole out of poaching pan and arrange on plate,
sprinkle with breadcrumbs mixture and cover with onion, capers and
mushrooms then grill under salamander for 2 seconds. Serve with parsley
and lemon.

James Macbeth
Skippers Bistro
1A Dock Place
Leith
Edinburgh

Halibut and Red Onions

6 oz halibut per portion or 4 oz for starter
medium size onion per portion
¼ bottle red wine
basil
seasoning
half clove chopped garlic

Pan fry halibut in a little butter and vegetable oil for approximately 2
minutes on each side until browned.
Remove and keep to one side for the moment.
In the same pan sautee the onions with half a clove of chopped garlic, a
pinch of chopped fresh basil and seasoning. Cook until soft and then add ¼
bottle red wine. Allow onions to cook into red wine to take up colour and
flavour until wine almost disappears.
Put halibut back into pan to reheat for a few minutes. Remove from pan and
serve on top of red onions.

Steven P Saunders
The Pink Geranium
Melbourn
Royston
Hertfordshire

Fillets of Sole Bonne-Femme

Serves 4

12 x 60g fillets of sole
salt and freshly ground pepper
100g butter
30g shallots
100g sliced button mushrooms
10cl white wine
20cl fish stock
20cl double cream
15g chopped parsley
4 turned mushrooms
4 fish fleurons

Season and fold the fillets of sole.
Grease a saucepan with a little butter and lay the fillets upon the top.
Sprinkle with white wine and add the shallots and sliced mushrooms.
Cover with a little fish stock and a greased paper.
Cook in the oven to taste, remove and dry the fish and keep warm.
Reduce the cooking liquor to a glaze form and add the double cream and
further reduce by one half.
Reheat the mushrooms and add the parsley to the sauce.
Mount the sauce with the butter and place the fish upon the serving dish.
Nappe the sauce over the fish and glaze under the salamander.
Garnish with the turned mushrooms and fish fleurons.
Serve immediately

Alan J Hill
The Gleneagles Hotel
Auchterarder
Perthshire
Scotland

Chilled Roulade of Smoked Salmon and Sole Mousse

Serves 8

Thin slices of best quality smoked salmon
12 oz lemon sole fillets
15 fl oz double cream
1 egg white
1 tsp finely chopped parsley
1 tsp finely chopped chervil
1 tsp finely chopped dill
nutmeg
5 fl oz natural yoghurt
1 tbsp sherry vinegar
½ cucumber

Cover a piece of tinfoil 12" x 8" with the thin slices of smoked salmon.
Liquidise the lemon sole fillets with the egg white, a good pinch of salt
and 5 fl oz double cream.
Pass through a fine sieve, then place in a bowl and set over ice to chill
for 5 minutes.
Carefully beat in most of the remaining cream, mixing thoroughly between
each addition.
At this point, test a little of the mousseline by poaching a teaspoonful in
hot water. Adjust consistency with more cream if the mousseline feels too
firm, then season with salt, pepper, nutmeg and fold in the herbs.
Spread an even layer of the mousseline over the smoked salmon, then
carefully roll up like a Swiss roll, twist the ends of the foil to seal.
Place in a large pot or fish kettle, cover with boiling water, then poach
very slowly for 30 minutes.
Remove and allow to cool then chill in the 'fridge.
Prepare the dressing by cutting half the cucumber into matchstick pieces
allow to drain for 10 minutes, then dry on a kitchen towel.
Mix the natural yoghurt with the sherry vinegar, then add to the cucumber.
With a sharp knife, cut through the foil into ½" slices, remove the foil
then arrange on a plate and serve with the cucumber dressing.

Bruce R Sangster
The Murrayshall
Country House Hotel, Restaurant and Golf Course
Scone
Perthshire
Scotland

POULTRY & GAME

Supreme of Chicken with Scallops, Wild Mushrooms and Creamy Curry Sauce

Serves 4

1½ tablespoons clarified butter
4 chicken supremes, skinned and trimmed of fat
salt and pepper
8 scallops, rinsed and drained
8 oz wild mushrooms, (Cepes, chanterelles, mousserons,
         morilles, girolles, etc), cleaned, trimmed and
         stalks scraped as necessary.
1 tablespoon chopped chives, to garnish.

For the sauce:

2 oz finely chopped shallot
½ bay leaf
1-2 teaspoon clarified butter
½ teaspoon good quality curry powder or paste
2 fl oz chicken stock
¼ pint double cream

First make the curry sauce. Fry the shallot and bay leaf in the butter
until golden brown. Add the curry powder or paste and dilute with the
chicken stock. Simmer for 10 minutes to reduce by about one-third until
the consistency is that of a paste. Add the cream and simmer, if it is too
thick, add a little more chicken stock, if too thin, reduce again. Pass
through a fine sieve and set aside.

Heat an ovenproof frying pan, add 1 tablespoon clarified butter and, when
moderately hot, add the seasoned supremes, outer side down. Agitate the
pan to prevent them sticking. When they begin to colour on the underside,
put the pan in the oven (230 deg C. 450 deg F Gas Mark 8), checking that
they are not sticking.

Grill the scallops for about 30 seconds to 1 minute on each side, making
sure that they are cooked right through but still juicy. Saute the
mushrooms in the remaining butter and season. Drain on kitchen paper and
keep warm.

After about five minutes remove the supremes from the oven; they should be
cooked through but juicy. Place on a serving dish, golden side up, with
the sauteed mushrooms. Run a thread of sauce over the mushrooms and on the
plate, avoiding the chicken. Add the scallops and sprinkle with chopped
chives.

Mr Smith
The Royal Oak Hotel
Yattendon
Newbury
Berkshire

Stuffed Breast of Chicken

Serves 4

For the stuffing you will need:
4 oz chopped cooked spinach
1 small finely chopped onion
1 oz fine breadcrumbs   )
2 oz ground hazelnuts   )   These can be done in a processor
salt and pepper
2 oz butter

4 boneless chicken breasts
aluminium foil

For the sauce:
1 pint chicken stock
¼ pint cream
1 tblsp chopped fresh tarragon
salt and pepper

Gently cook the chopped onion in the butter until translucent, add the
breadcrumbs and hazels and on a low heat, cook until the crumbs and hazels
are golden brown, remove from the heat, stir in the spinach and season,
leave to cool.
Prepare the chicken breasts by slicing a pocket in each one in order to
fill with the stuffing, make sure the pockets are deep enough to take a
reasonable amount of stuffing. Fill each breast with stuffing and fold the
flap of meat over so that the stuffing is covered, season each breast.
Butter four pieces of foil and wrap the breasts up, not too tightly and put
on a tray ready to bake at 450 deg F for 15 minutes.
For the sauce, put the chicken stock in a pan, and over a fast flame,
reduce it until about 6 tablespoons are left, (keep a careful eye on it as
it reduces rather quickly) add the cream and bring back to the boil, remove
from the heat, add the tarragon and seasoning, the sauce is now ready.
Check the chicken, especially the top end of the breasts, if it is firm to
the touch (through the foil) then they are ready.
Carefully remove each breast from the foil, remembering that each package
will contain some hot liquid, slice each breast into three on a slant so
that the stuffing is visible, dress on a large plate or dish and pour the
sauce over.

Sonja Kidney
The Marsh Goose
Moreton in Marsh
Gloucestershire

Fillet of Goosnargh Chicken studded with Truffle

Serves 1

7 oz breast of Goosnargh chicken
chicken consomme
50 ml dry sparkling wine
fresh truffle
splash of brandy
25 g butter
50 ml double cream
50 ml creme fraiche
fresh chervil

Take the breast of chicken and score with a knife making a cross-like pattern on top to a depth of 3 mm.

Lard with a Juliene of Truffle.

Gently poach in consomme and wine.

Take out chicken and keep warm.

Reduce stock by half, add cream and creme fraiche, monte with butter, correct seasoning.

Place chicken on plate, coat with sauce place spatzli alongside, garnish with chervil.

SPATZLI

20 portions

1 kg plain flour
6 eggs
6 dl water
mixed herbs and garlic

Mix all ingredients together, whip till bubbles appear.

Cook in boiling water with oil, refresh.

Fry in butter until crispy.

Nigel Haworth
Northcote Manor
Northcote Road
Langho
Blackburn
Lancashire

Breast of Chicken Stuffed with Leek Mousse

Serves 4

5 x 6-7 oz chicken breasts
2 green top leeks
10 fl oz whipping cream (including sauce)
3 fl oz chicken stock
3 fl oz white wine
salt and pepper

Cut leeks into 2 inch pieces, wash and cook in boiling salted water for 1
minute and refresh in cold water and set aside.
Take away all bone and sinew from the chicken breasts and put one aside for
mousse.
Split the 4 chicken breasts open by pulling back the fillet making a cut
the opposite side.
Bat out each breast lightly until they are of an even thickness.
Place remaining chicken breast in a food processor with salt and pepper and
blend and then add 4 fl oz of the cream and blend again.

To Put Together

Lay out chicken breasts place a piece of dark leek (flat piece) on each
breast followed by a layer of mousse and then a piece of solid white leek,
cover this with more mousse and finally encase with another piece of dark
leek.
Wrap the fillet over leek and then the other side.
For best results wrap in cling film tightly and place in fridge for at
least two hours.

For the Sauce

Place chicken stock and white wine in a saucepan and simmer for 1 minute
and add about 4 oz of the remaining leek and the remaining cream and salt
and pepper.

Simmer for a further 2 minutes and then liquidise.

NOTE: Chicken breast can either by cooked by frying in a
        little oil and butter or by leaving in cling film
        and placing in shallow water and placing in the oven.
        Cooking time 15 minutes, approximately.

John Mann
Montagu Arms
Palace Lane
Beaulieu
Hampshire

82

Chicken, Bacon and Banana Wellington

Take four boneless chicken breasts and seal in hot fat very briefly on all sides. Make a cut in the centre, the full length of the breast, and stuff with thin slices of banana. Paint over the banana with lemon juice. Season the breasts with freshly ground salt and pepper. Wrap a rasher of lean, rindless, smoked bacon around each breast. Encase each breast in its own puff pastry parcel, and rest in 'fridge.

To cook: place in the centre of a hot oven for approximately 20 minutes. Accompany with banana chutney.

Joy Hadley
Rumbles Cottage Restaurant
Braintree Road
Felstead
Essex

Chicken and Lime Rice

4 supreme chicken	¼ bottle dry white wine
1 oz butter	½ pint double cream
2 oz plain flour	2 limes
1 pint strong chicken stock	½ lb rice
5 rashers streaky bacon	

Gently brown supremes in pan on top of cooker – then place in oven for 30 minutes on Gas mark 6.

Sauce:
Melt butter in pan and add flour whisking until roux has been formed. Bring chicken stock to the boil and gently add to the roux, whisking continuously until smooth mixture. Add white wine and double cream and season. The sauce is now ready.

Garnish:
Finely chop bacon and fry until crisp. Leave to go cold.

Rice:
Peel zest off limes and finely chop. Juice the limes and while cooking rice add both the chopped peel and juice.

To serve:
Place supremes on bed of rice. Cover supremes with cream sauce and garnish with chopped bacon.

Oliver Godfrey
Le Grandgousier
15 Western Street
Brighton
Sussex

Turkey/Chicken Kiev Balls

Mince (preferably in a processor) approximately 12 oz of turkey/chicken breasts (raw).
Put in a large bowl and add 2 - 3 cloves of crushed garlic.
Add 2 egg whites (unbeaten) and 1 oz of soft but not melted butter and mix thoroughly together.
Roll into large marble size balls.
Coat with flour, egg and breadcrumbs and deep fry for a few minutes (3-5 minutes) in a medium-hot fryer.

Serve.

Steven P Saunders
The Pink Geranium
Melbourn
Royston
Hertfordshire

Poulet Saute Safrane

Serves 4

6 oz butter
oil as required
2 x 3.5 lb chickens, cut into 16 equal pieces
salt and pepper to taste
2 large onions, finely chopped
good pinch Saffron, leaves preferred not ground
½ bottle white wine
2 pints veal stock, slightly thickened, or use stock cubes
½ pint double cream
parsley, chopped, to garnish.

Heat butter and just enough oil to prevent burning in a thick bottomed pan.
Season the chicken with salt and pepper and saute the pieces until golden brown. Remove chicken, strain fat and wipe out pan.
Return fat to pan, add onions and sweat without colouring them. Add saffron and white wine and reduce by half. Add stock, return chicken, cover and cook for 20 minutes. If necessary, add more stock.
Remove chicken and skim off any grease from top of sauce. Reduce sauce if needed to get correct flavouring. Add cream and stir until sauce returns to boil.

Dress chicken on serving dish, cover with sauce and sprinkle with chopped parsley. Serving suggestion: serve with boiled or plain rice.

Richard Shepherd
Langans Brasserie
Stratton Street
Piccadilly
London

84

Layered Quail Tartlet with Red Wine Sauce

Serves 4

4 x 4 inch shortcrust pastry tartlets, pre baked
2 teaspoons rowan jelly
4 quail
4-6 oz hispi or savoy cabbage, finely shredded
1 oz pine nuts
2 Bartlett pears, poached in light red wine syrup
4 oz butter
seasoning.

For Sauce

1/3 pint red burgundy
½ pint game stock
½ pint veal stock
2 oz unsalted butter
seasoning

Peel and poach pears in a light red wine syrup, quarter and fan out.

Lightly cook the shredded cabbage, season, add butter and toss with the pine nuts. Keep warm.

Roast quails in a hot oven Gas mark 6 / 400 deg F / 220 deg C until pink; take off breasts and legs, keep warm to one side.

Reduce the red wine until syrupy, add the game stock and reduce to one-third. Add the veal stock and reduce again to one-third. Reserve and keep warm.

Warm the tartlets and spread with rowan jelly. Add the cabbage and pine nut mixture, arrange the pears on top of this, then add the breasts and legs of the quail.

Place on warm plates and finish the sauce with knobs of butter. Pour sauce around the tartlets, garnish with sprigs of fresh thyme and serve immediately.

Colin John Bussey
The Gleneagles Hotel
Auchterarder
Perthshire
Scotland

Quails in Potato Nests

Potato Nests (one per person)

Peel and grate potato finely. Do not wash it when grated as the starch helps to hold it together.

Put grated potato in a very hot pan with a little oil and fry till golden
brown and turn over and fry again.
If you have a basket press put the potato into the press and plunge into a
deep fat fryer.

The Quail (2 quails per person)

Buy your quails de-boned from your butcher/supermarket. Make a stuffing
such as:

1 dessertspoon of bechamel sauce
1 dessertspoon breadcrumbs
1 clove garlic, pressed or finely chopped
1 dessertspoon sausage meat
finely chopped mushrooms
sprinkling of fresh garden herbs
seasoning

The above is sufficient for 2 quails.

Fill each quail with the stuffing and bake in a moderate oven (gas 5/6) for
15 minutes.

Serve with a rich red wine and port wine sauce.

Steven P Saunders
The Pink Geranium
Melbourn
Royston
Hertfordshire

Salmis De Palombe

Serves 6

6 plump pigeons
6 thin slices streaky bacon
2 carrots, 1 celeriac, white part of 2 leeks, 4 shallots
    and 6 mushrooms, all finely chopped.
1 tablespoon flour (preferably potato flour)
1 generous glass red wine
4 pints (2.25 1) water
½ head garlic, crushed
1 bay leaf, 3 sprigs each thyme and parsley
1 tablespoon tomato puree
1 dessertspoon mixed, whole spices (pepper, nutmeg,
    coriander and cloves)

Place the pigeons with a rasher of bacon on each in a very hot oven for 7
minutes. Remove and allow to cool. When cold, remove the breast from each
side by cutting along the length of the breast bone and set aside. Roughly
chop the pigeon carcasses and saute in a little goose/duck fat or olive

oil. Add the chopped vegetables, stirring continuously to soften without browning. Sprinkle over the flour and stir a couple of times.

Add the wine, then the water. Add the herbs, spices and tomato puree and simmer gently, covered, for 4 hours or overnight (do not boil).

Pass everything through a fine sieve, then liquidize in a blender. Reheat gently with the pigeon breasts, adding red wine to thin if necessary. Salt to taste.

Slice each pigeon breast in half along its axis and serve on croutons fried in oil, with sauce over. Serve with green cabbage, sautee of baby onions and Pommes Anna.

Nicholas Blacklock
La Bastide
50 Greek Street
London W1

Breast of Pheasant with Apple and Pink Peppercorn Compote

Serves 4

4 breasts of pheasant (2 birds and trimmings)
2 large cooking apples
pink peppercorns

Either bone out the pheasant breasts yourself or ask you butcher to do it for you. Boil up carcasses and legs to make stock. Lightly seal breast in a pan with a little butter and oil, fresh rosemary, ground black pepper and salt. Wrap each breast in tin foil with a sprig of rosemary and set aside. Peel and dice the apples. Add a few pink peppercorns and lightly heat with a couple of drops of lemon juice until mushy. Place breast in hot oven mark 7 for 20 minutes. Reduce pheasant stock right down until like a syrup. Place breast on plate and slice thinly. Pour over a little of reduced stock and a spoonful of apple. Serve immediatley

Nicholas and Nicola Hayward
Seaview Hotel and Restaurant
The High Street
Seaview
Isle of Wight

Wild Duck Breast Roasted and Served with Damson Compote, The Leg Casseroled with Juniper and Orange

Serves 4

2 wild ducks (2 portions per duck)
a little seasoned flour
1 dessertspoon tomato puree
1 tablespoon redcurrant jelly
zest of one orange
6 crushed juniper berries
1 bay leaf
4 sprigs of fresh thyme
½ pint of red wine
¾ pint of chicken or veal stock
1 onion
1 carrot
1 stick of celery
parsley stalks
clove garlic

Remove the legs and thighs from the duck and dip in seasoned flour. Heat a little oil in a pan, brown the legs and remove. Sweat the onion, garlic, carrot and celery in the pan, pour in the wine and reduce, add the veal or chicken stock, tomato puree, orange zest and crushed juniper berries, season.

Add the legs and herbs, gently cook until tender, remove and sieve the liquid, add 1 tablespoon reducrrant jelly, reduce and check for seasoning. If desired you can thicken slightly with a little arrowroot. Skim the surface of the sauce, finish with a knob of butter.

While the legs are casseroling, roast the breast in a hot oven, smear the breasts with softened butter and baste frequently, cook for 20 or 30 minutes depending on how rare or well done you like your meat. To serve remove the breast from the bone and arrange on your plate with the sauce poured over the leg. Serve with pickled damsons or damson compote, garnishing with a sprig of fresh marjoram or other available herb.

Stephen Smith
The Belvedere Hotel
19 North Park Road
Bradford
West Yorkshire

Wild Duck 'En Croute' with Port and Cinnamon Sauce

Serves 6

The Pate:
4 oz Breast of Wild Duck
4 oz lean pork
4 oz pork fat
2 tablespoons of reduced gelatinous wild duck stock
a little port
a little brandy
spice/quatre espices
seasoning

Puff Pastry

Sauce:
reduced stock
stick of cinnamon
port
two shallots
1 oz unsalted butter

Mince finely the meat and fat, add reduced stock (see below), alcohol and seasoning. Test by cooking a little bit of Pate for tasting. Put in the 'fridge.

Roll out six circles of pastry 1/16 inch thick and 4½ inches diameter. Repeat for six circles of 1½ inch diameter.

Put the large circle in floured cup or salad bowl. Add meat in centre with small circle on top.

Glaze the edges of the inside of the big circle with egg and the top of the small circle. Fold the big circle onto the small circle and seal, enclosing the meat in.

Turn the Pate out and shape with your hands. Rest in the 'fridge.

Make the sauce: To make a brown stock, roast the chopped up wild duck carcasses. Half way through add some vegetables (onion, celery, carrot), in order to caramelize them and add some tomato puree 10 minutes before the end. Put the bones in a saucepan, cover with water or (ideally) veal stock, boil, skim, add bouquet garni, turn the heat down and simmer for four hours skimming from time to time. Pass the stock through a sieve.

Reduce stock down half-way skimming all the time. (use some of this for the Pate).

Break up the cinnamon into small pieces. Sweat with chopped shallots for two minutes, deglaze with Port, reduce by half, add reduced stock and again, reduce 'til the taste is good. Add a little arrowroot if necessary to thicken.

Glaze the Pate with egg and make two small holes in the top. Cook at Gas 5 (375 deg F) on a heavy tray lined with greaseproof paper, for 15 minutes, until the pastry is golden brown and inside cooked. Test by putting skewer through the middle to determine the temperature. It should be hot in the middle.

Whisk unsalted butter into the sauce, put it onto a plate and arrange Pate on top.

David and Mary Adlard
Adlard's Restaurant
79 Upper St Giles Street
Norwich
Norfolk

Duck Breast and Raspberry Vinegar Sauce

1½ lb Duckling

Remove Duck legs and set aside. Remove breast with bone intact. Roast carcass with vegetables, add 2 pints chicken stock and 2 tablespoons of raspberry wine vinegar, and 4 oz fresh or frozen raspberries, bring to the boil and simmer to reduce.

Roast breast in one piece in very hot oven till pink inside - 15 minutes approximately. Strain and reduce sauce to about 4 tablespoons, it should coat the back of a spoon.

Carve breasts from bone and slice length-ways, put small amount of sauce on plate, lay meat across and garnish with either fried pears or small raspberry tartlet.

The legs can be crisply roasted and served after the breast with a salad.

Stephen and Anne Frost
The Stonor Arms
Stonor
Nr Henley-on-Thames
Oxfordshire

Crispy Duck and Salad Frisee

Make a delicate salad from predominantly curly endive, Belgian endive, Radiccio. Trim the meat from a crisply roasted duck leg. Chop roughly and place on the salad. Dress with green herb mustard vinaigrette.

Mr Smith
The Royal Oak Hotel
Yattendon
Newbury
Berkshire

Fillet of Hare served with a Timbale of Wild Mushrooms

Serves 4

1 filleted loin of hare (with all silver skin and sinew removed)
1 pint hare sauce
4 small strands of redcurrants with leaf
4 mushroom timbale
4 fleuron (fill with foie gras if available)
seasoning
¼ pint red wine
4 oz redcurrants

Season and lightly pan fry hare to seal, finish in warm oven until pink 5-7 minutes.
Deglaze cooking pan with the wine and redcurrants, add sauce, boil until it reduces to a good flavour, strain, reboil and dress on plate, place timbale on centre left of plate.
Slice and dress hare on centre right of plate.
Place fleuron, redcurrants and leaf bottom centre.

MAKE SURE THE HARE IS COOKED PINK AND NOT DRIED UP.
CHECK THE DISH IS HOT.

Hare Sauce

8 lbs hare bones
2 lbs mirepoix
8 oz red currant jelly
4 oz butter
4 oz flour
8 pints game stock
1 pint red wine
bunch thyme
seasoning
4 oz bitter sweet chocolate, grated.

Brown bones in butter, add mirepoix.
Add flour and cook out.
Stir in red wine and cold stock, bring to the boil, simmer for 1 hour.
Season, add jelly and thicken with chocolate.
Strain through a fine chinois.

Fleuron

Makes 24

10 oz full puff pastry
egg wash
seeds, poppy, sesame, caraway
seasoning
filling if required.

Fleuron are small baked pieces of puff pastry cut into shapes (2 inches, round, diamond, crescent, rectangle) and egg wash to give a high gloss and can be filled with savoury cream, mousse, foie gras or left plain.
Roll out pastry to 1/8th inch, egg wash, draw fork across to make a line, season and cut into the desired shapes. At this time seeds may be sprinkled on if required.
Place on baking sheet and bake 210 C until golden brown and dry.
If you are required to fill them allow to cool, cut in half and place filling in centre.

Timbale of Wild Mushroom

Serves 4

2 oz finely chopped wild mushrooms
1 tblsp creme fraiche
1 egg
seasoning
turned mushroom for garnish

Work all ingredients together and place in small timbale moulds lined with clig film.
Steam for 9 minutes.
Taste before cooking, seasoning.

HARE SAUCE CAN BE MADE THE DAY BEFORE.
FLEURONS CAN BE MADE BEFOREHAND.
MUSHROOM TIMBALE CAN BE PREPARED A LITTLE EARLIER AND REHEATED BUT YOU WILL LOSE A LITTLE OF THE LIGHTNESS.

Nick Buckingham
Cavendish Hotel
Baslow
Derbyshire

Rabbit in Cider with Prunes

A good simple rustic stew

Serves 2 - 3

4 rabbit joints
1 tablespoons seasoned flour
8 oz (225g) streaky bacon or pancetta (cured spiced belly pork)
1-2 tablespoons sunflower or peanut (groundnut) oil
2 large onions, peeled, halved and thinly sliced to form crescents
1 clove garlic, peeled and chopped
10 fl oz (300ml) cider or dry white or red wine
10 fl oz (300ml) good homemade stock
1 bunch fresh herbs (bay leaf, parsley, thyme)
Pinch of salt

Freshly ground black pepper
4 oz (110g) stoned prunes
croutons and chopped parsley to garnish

First wash the rabbit joints and pat dry with kitchen paper. Dust in
seasoned flour and wrap each piece in a strip of bacon or pancetta,
securing with wooden cocktail sticks.
Heat the oil in a heavy frying pan and gently brown the onions in it.
Towards the end of their cooking time add the garlic. Transfer them to a
flameproof casserole and set aside. Then brown the rabbit pieces all over
in the frying pan and add these to the casserole too. Pour the cider or
wine and stock over the rabbit, add the herbs, salt and pepper and gently
heat until barely simmering. Cover tightly and continue simmering very
gently for 1 - 1½ hours or until the rabbit is tender. Fifteen minutes
before the end of the cooking time, add the prunes.
To serve, arrange the rabbit pieces on an attractive shallow platter and
keep warm while you quickly boil the sauce to reduce and thicken it
somewhat. Pour it all over the rabbit and strew with croutons and lots of
chopped parsley.

Susan Hicks. After her very successful BBC TV Series and accompanying book
The Fish Course, Susan has now written The Main Course.

Terrine of Rabbit with Pork and Prunes

One terrine to serve 8 - 10 people

One wild rabbit
1 lb belly pork
8 oz smoked bacon
4 oz soaked and stoned prunes (soaked in brandy is luxurious!)
Salt, pepper, ½ clove garlic, ½ small onion
½ oz juniper berries
One egg

Remove saddle meat from rabbit in two strips. Mince leg meat with pork and
bacon in fine mincer. Mix in remaining ingredients except prunes. Put one
third of the mixture in bottom of terrine. Lay half the saddle meat
lengthways down the terrine with a layer of prunes between two strips of
meat. Put next third of mixture on top and repeat process using up all the
mixture. Cook in bain-marie for one hour in low oven.

Allow to cool with light weight over terrine. Do not discard juices
surrounding terrine which will set as a delicious jelly. When cold turn
out, slice and serve with pickled fruits or chutneys.

Stephen and Penny Ross
Homewood Park Hotel
Hinton Charterhouse
Bath
Avon

Poached Breast of Guinea Fowl

served with a Rich Port and Fresh Cherries Sauce

Breast of Guinea Fowl (say 4-5 oz per person)
Onions, carrots, leeks (not celery or peppers)
chicken stock
white wine

Place the guinea fowl in a dish with the vegetables (roughly chopped) and a
little chicken stock with white wine. Cover with tin foil and place in the
oven (gas mark 7, 220 C, 425 F) Leave for 15-20 minutes.

Sauce:

3-4 tblsp port
2 shallots (finely chopped)
2 dessertspoons redcurrant jelly
white wine
1 tblsp honey
12-14 stoned cherries

Place port and shallots in a small saucepan, bring to a gently boil and
reduce. Add the redcurrant jelly, a splash of white wine, the honey and
stoned cherries. Cook for 10-15 minutes on low heat.

Note:- the cherries can be replaced with nectarines or french plums.

Steven P Saunders
The Pink Geranium
Melbourn
Royston
Hertfordshire

Pintadeaux MacArthur

Guinea fowl MacArthur style

Serves 6 - 8

2 young guinea fowl
¼ gill brandy
¾ gill white wine
14 oz fresh pineapple
3½ gills of demiglace
2 oz butter
1¾ oz chopped almonds
10oz rice (patna)
4 oz larding bacon

Bard the guinea fowl with larding bacon, (i.e. cover the fowl with bacon) and tie with string, then fry in butter so that they are still pink. Remove from pan. Pour off the frying butter and flambee the pan residue with brandy, (i.e. pour the spirit over the fowl and set it alight). Reduce with white wine (i.e. boil rapidly, uncovered), then add the finely diced pineapple and simmer together for a few minutes. Add the demiglace, boil a little longer and season with a pinch of cayenne pepper. Carve the guinea fowl, pour the sauce with the pineapple over them and sprinkle with chopped roasted almonds.

Serve with rice cooked with saffron.

Karl Wadsack
The Three Lions
Stuckton
Fordingbridge
Hampshire

Guinea Fowl with Green Peppercorns and Spinach Cakes

Serves 4

2 guinea fowl
1 oz green peppercorns
2 oz chopped shallots
2 limes
¾ pint double cream
1 oz butter
salt and pepper
2 oz sugar
3 fl oz white wine
10 fl oz white guinea fowl stock

Spinach Cakes:
  100g spinach puree
  nutmeg to taste
  salt and pepper
  4 egg whites
  4 egg yolks
  10g flour

Remove breasts and legs, take bone out of legs.
Make stock with bones
Season the guinea and saute, when cooked remove from the pan and keep warm.
Deglace the pan with white wine and reduce, add sugar and water and make a caramel; add half peppercorns (crushed) to sauce.
Add guinea stock and reduce by ¾. Add double cream and reduce to right consistency.
Zest both limes and blanch the zest for 10 minutes to remove bitterness and refresh.
Add juice of one lime to the sauce and taste (the other lime is to be cut in segments for garnish).
Pass sauce through a strainer.
Place guinea fowl in a dish and pour sauce over and around.
Garnish with green peppercorns and spinach cakes, lime segments and the caramelized zest.

Spinach Cakes

Mix spinach puree with the flour and egg yolk and season with salt, pepper and nutmeg.
Whisk egg whites until they are very stiff, gently fold egg whites into spinach.
Spread mix onto a shallow tray, wrap in cling film.
Cook in a waterbath for approximately 10 minutes and allow to cool, then cut into shapes.

Keith Stanley
The Ritz
Piccadilly
London

Medallions of Maize Fed Guinea Fowl

with a Pistachio Nut and Chive Filling

Serves 4

4 guinea fowl supremes (the dish can be done using chicken supremes)
2 oz chicken breast
1 carrot
1 oz pistachio nuts blanched and skinned
fresh chives
½ pint double cream

For the sauce:
1 pint stock made from the carcass of guinea fowl or chicken
¼ pint red wine
¼ pint ruby port
1 onion
cold butter to finish

Remove the fillets from the supremes and place with the chicken meat in a
liquidiser. Process them remove and rub through a sieve. Place in a bowl
and set over ice with a little salt and gradually work in the double cream.
Allow to rest.
Prepare a fine dice of carrot and blanch in boiling salted water.
Finely chop the pistachio nuts.
Mix the carrot, nuts and chives into the mousse, adjust the seasoning.
Bat out the supremes with a meat hammer between plastic sheets.
Butter 4 sheets of tin foil and place one supreme on each sheet, season
with salt and pepper.
Add some of the mousse down the centre of the supremes then carefully roll
up and secure in the foil, allow to rest.
Meanwhile prepare the light sauce by browning the onion which should be
finely sliced then add the stock and reduce quickly by half.
Add both port and red wine and again reduce by half.
Strain and pass through a fine muslin, keep warm.
In a thick bottomed pan with a little oil seal the tin foil parcels and
place in the oven gas 6-7 approximately 400 F for 8-10 minutes. Remove and
allow to rest.
Finish the sauce by bringing to the boil and adding cold butter. Do not
reboil as sauce will separate.
Remove the foil from the supremes and carve into 8-9 thin slices, arrange
on hot plates and nap with the sauce.
Serve with vegetables of your choice.

Bruce R Sangster
The Murrayshall
Country House Hotel, Restaurant and Golf Course
Scone
Perthshire
Scotland

Traditional Roast Grouse

Serves 2
2 grouse (oven ready)
2 slices streaky bacon
2 croutons (fried in butter)
½ diced carrot
2 sticks celery
1 small leek
½ small onion
1/6th pint red wine
½ pint veal stock
parsley
bay leaf

Farce au Gratin
30g chicken livers
30g grouse livers
15g shallots
25g mushrooms
30g pork fat
thyme
seasoning

Farce au gratin

Method:
Fry shallots and thyme with the pork fat, add the livers and mushrooms and fry over full heat until the livers are half cooked and cool on ice.
When they are cool pass through a food processor or fine mincer, check seasoning and place some of the farce moulded onto the crouton.

To cook the grouse:

Cover the grouse with streaky bacon and tie loosely to keep the bacon on.
Melt a little fat in a small roasting tin and seal the birds on all sides.
Season. Place in a hot oven at 200C, 400F, Gas mark 6 for approximately 30 minutes.
Once the grouse has cooked, remove from the oven and leave to rest for 5 minutes.
Remove the grease from the roasting tray and place the tray over heat. Add the roughly diced vegetables and fry to colour.
Once the grouse has rested you can either serve it on the bone or remove the breasts etc from the carcass. Chop the carcass and add the vegetables to make a sauce.
After you have fried the vegetables and bones, add a little red wine, a few parsley stalks and bay leaf, add ½ pint veal stock and reduce the sauce to the required strength as grouse can be very strong in flavour when well matured.
Pass the sauce and serve with the grouse, the reheated crouton, bread sauce, and it is traditional to serve fried breadcrumbs on the side with some game chips (fried potatoes), and watercress.

Ron Maxfield
Cliveden
Taplow
Berkshire

MEAT

Noisette D'Agneau

Serves 1

1 canon of lamb at 160g cooked pink, in olive oil
1 lambs kidney, cut in a butterfly with the fat removed, cooked pink
   in olive oil
2 spoons marmalade of onions, made as follows:
   2lbs finely sliced onions sweated off in 4 tablespoons of olive oil.
   Add 4 oz caster sugar, 10 fl oz of white wine vinegar, 4 cloves, 2 bay
   leaves, 1 teaspoon ground black pepper, 1 teaspoon salt, 2 tablespoons
   tomato puree and a pinch of cayenne pepper
   Cook gently for 1 hour after which check the seasoning

4 pieces of saute potatoes, cooked from raw until golden brown, in olive
   oil
Batons of vegetables consisting of carrot, celeriac, courgette and white
   radish, blanched in water and then glaced
Small dice of courgette and tomato fried in olive oil
1 sauce boat of jus d'agneau perfumed with rosemary
4 sprigs rosemary

Place the marmalade of onions in the middle of the plate with the kidney on
top and the courgette and tomato inside the kidney.
Place the potatoes at four equal points on the plate and cut the lamb, once
cooked, into four equal pieces and place on top of the potatoes.

The batons of vegetables are then put in between the pieces of lamb and
then the sauce is put on the plate only.

Place sprigs of rosemary on top of the lamb.

Kevin Cape
The Bell Inn
Aston Clinton
Buckinghamshire

Meli-Melo D'Agneau aux Gousses D'Ail et Romarin

(A simple panache of lamb with baked garlic and rosemary)

Serves 4

4 x 120g boned loin of lamb (no fat)
4 small braised lamb tongues
4 lambs' kidneys
240g lamb sweetbreads (well blanched)
75ml white wine
8 large cloves of garlic (in their skin)
10g garlic puree
1 bunch fresh rosemary
30 g shallots
50g butter
250 ml lamb stock (made from bones)
salt, pepper

For the sauce:
Sweat chopped shallots, garlic puree and a little washed rosemary in butter, deglace with white wine. Reduce, add lamb stock and reduce until correct consistency. Pass through a muslin strainer and finish with butter.
Saute the loins of lamb, cook in oven with a little rosemary until very pink.
Slice the kidneys into 3/8 inch slices, remove centre fat and saute in oil very quickly. Saute the prepared and blanched sweetbreads in butter, slice as for the kidneys.
Heat the lambs' tongues in their braising liquor and slice lengthways approximately ¼ inch thick.
Bake the garlic cloves in their skins. Remove when soft and peel off skins.

To Serve:
Slice the loin lengthways and fan it out on individual plates. Arrange the sweetbreads, tongue and kidneys attractively around. Cordon the meat with the sauce. Garnish with the baked garlic cloves and sprigs of buttered rosemary.

A mousseline of celeriac or spinach accompanies this dish and may either be served on the dish itself, or on a small plate alongside.

Serve immediately.

Paul Gaylor
Inigo Jones
14 Garrick Street
London

Babotie

Serves 10

3 slices white bread
1½ pints (900 ml) milk
2½ lb (1.25 kg) cooked, minced lamb
2 medium-sized onions, chopped
2 apples, chopped
3 oz (75g) butter
2 heaped tablespoons curry powder
2 tablespoons chutney
2 oz (50g) chopped almonds
1 oz (25g) raisins
3 tablespoons vinegar or lemon juice
salt and black pepper

For the top

3 eggs
salt and black pepper
lemon leaves or bay leaves

Soak the bread in the milk, squeeze dry and place in a mixing bowl, with the minced lamb.
Set the oven to 180 deg C / 350 deg F / gas mark 4. Grease an oven-proof dish.
Fry the onion and apple slowly in the butter. Add the curry powder and cook for a further minute.
Mix the apple and onion with the lamb and bread, add the chutney, almonds, raisins and vinegar or lemon juice. Season with salt and black pepper.
Pile into the greased dish and place in the warm oven for about 10 minutes to form a slight crust on top.
Meanwhile, mix the eggs with the milk in which the bread has been soaked. Season with salt and pepper.
Pour this over the meat, place the lemon or bay leaves on top and continue to bake until the custard has set and browned. (about 30 minutes)

Pru Leith, owner of Leith's Restaurant and Leith's School of Food and Wine, both in London. She has also written many cookery books and articles in magazines such as Taste.

102

Sri Lankan Curry

Sometimes – however much we may want to be truly authentic in our cooking – time forces us into compromise. And this was never more so than in the art of cooking curry. Men who never have to do any other cooking are prepared to spend days, marinating, grinding spices and so forth, and even find all this relaxing. It's quite another matter for the busy housewife.

Here's a curry, from what used to be known as Ceylon, that strikes a balance between an authentic flavour and not involving too much fuss.

It makes interesting use of coconut; so first a word about them. I've heard it said the best way to break them is to drop them from a great height on to the kitchen floor! But in the plastic-floored 90's I think a hammer is best. Crack the nut into manageable pieces and then use a knife to separate the flesh from the shell. But don't forget to make a couple of holes through the soft indentations at the base first, with a skewer or clean screwdriver, to drain off the milk (and reserve it).

Serves 6

1½ lb (700g) chuck steak (cut into cubes)
2 onions (chopped small)
3 tablespoons oil
1 large clove garlic (crushed)
1½ heaped tablespoon flour
1 tablspoon Madras curry powder
3 oz (75g) coconut (grated)
3 oz (75g) creamed coconut (available in packets)
the milk from 1 coconut
1¼ pints (720ml) approximately, stock
1-inch cinnamon stick
6 cardamon pods (crushed)
1 teaspoon fenugreek
salt and freshly-milled pepper

To garnish
2 small onions (quartered then spearated into layers)
2 hardboiled eggs (quartered)

Pre-heat oven to 300 deg F, 150 deg C, gas mark 2.

First heat 2 tablespoons oil in a large casserole, then add the onions and garlic and cook gently to soften for 5 minutes. Next heat 1 tablespoon of oil in a frying pan and quickly brown the cubes of meat over a high heat.

Sprinkle the flour and curry powder over the onions in the casserole and stir to soak up the juice, then cook gently for 2 minutes. Now pour the coconut milk into a measuring jug and make up to 1½ pints with beef stock, then slowly pour this into the casserole, stirring all the time. Next stir in the fresh and creamed coconut (grated) and transfer the browned meat to the casserole. Finally add the spices and salt and pepper.

Bring up to simmering point, then cover and cook in the centre of the oven for 2 hours. Five minutes before the end of the cooking time, stir the hard-boiled eggs and onion pieces into the curry to warm through (the onions are not meant to be cooked).

Finally a traditional accompaniment.

Coconut Sambal

Quite simply, grate the flesh of half a coconut and a medium onion into a bowl. Sprinkle in ¼ teaspoon chilli powder, 2 teaspoons lemon juice and ¼ teaspoon salt, and stir to get everything nicely blended. Chill slightly till needed.

This recipe was sent to us by Delia Smith who I am sure needs no introduction.

Sliced Roast Fillet of Lamb with a Honey and Sherry Sauce

Serves 4

4 fillets of lamb from the saddle, trimmed
3 oz butter
4 oz fresh pasta
seasonal baby vegetables

Sauce:

2 medium shallots
1 tblsp sherry vinegar
1 tblsp honey
1 pint lamb stock

Sweat shallots in butter, add honey and caramelise. Deglaze with vinegar and reduce. Add lamb stock and reduce by half.
Season and pass through sieve.
Remove any skin from fillets and tie with string. Brush with clarified butter and a little honey. Season.
Seal in hot pan until brown and roast in hot oven for 3-5 minutes.
Transfer to dish and rest for 10 minutes.
Cook pasta until al dente in boiling, salted water.
Place pasta in centre of plate.
Slice lamb and arrange around pasta.
Pour on sauce and garnish with baby vegetables.

Thierry Lepretre-Granet
Whitechapel Manor
South Molton
North Devon

Lamb Cutlets with Wild Rice and Mild Curry Sauce

Serves 4

12 lamb cutlets, trimmed
3 oz butter

Wild Rice:
5 oz wild rice
1 sprig thyme
½ bay leaf
8 fl oz chicken stock
½ dessert apple, diced
3 oz raisins, soaked

Curry Sauce:

1 dessert apple, diced
½ banana, sliced
2 oz butter
1 oz shallots
2 oz button mushrooms
1 oz mild curry powder
1 tblsp freshly grated coconut
¼ pint white wine
¾ pint chicken stock
½ pint double cream

Place wild rice, thyme, bay leaf and salt with chicken stock in saucepan.
Bring to boil and simmer gently for about 1 hour. Drain and refresh.
Sweat shallots and mushrooms in butter. Add wine and reduce to a liquor.
Add banana, apple, coconut, curry powder and chicken stock.
Reduce by half and add cream. Cook over slow heat until it reaches
required consistency. Season and sieve.
Brown lamb in butter on both sides, keeping flesh pink. Season and rest
for 10 minutes.
Saute apple and raisins in butter.
Add wild rice to heat through.
Cook spinach in butter for few minutes. Season.
Pour sauce on plate and arrange cutlets, rice and spinach.

Thierry Lepretre-Granet
Whitechapel Manor
South Molton
North Devon

105

Lancashire Hot Pot

Serves 4

4 good thick lean lamb chump chops
4 potatoes, peeled
2 carrots   )
2 sticks celery)   all very, very finely diced
2 onions   )
1 leek   )
½ clove crushed garlic
2 good sprigs fresh rosemary
1 pint reduced juiced dark lamb stock
sprinkling of chopped parsley
2-3 oz butter for cooking

To make this you will need to brown the chops in, preferably, lamb fat
which can be made by taking any excess fat off the chops, rendering it down
with a touch of water and clarifying. If you don't have time for this,
just use a little of the butter. Brown them on both sides and place on one
side. Slice the potatoes into round slices about 2 mm thick add this also
to the lamb fat with a bit of the picked rosemary and fry off in the
butter, allowing a little bit of colour. Place these to one side. Lay the
four chops into a casseroling pan and take the finely chopped vegetables
and sweat in a little butter with the garlic and some more of the rosemary.
Spoon this mixture onto the top of each of the chops, arrange the sliced
potatoes on top into a neat pattern on each chop, so, in effect, what we
have is a lamb chop on the base, which has been sauteed, spreading the
finely diced vegetables with the garlic and rosemary and the sliced
potatoes on top. Pour over the reduced stock and place on the stove and
allow to simmer. Pop into the oven and these will take about 35 - 40
minutes to cook, keeping them nice and tender in a medium oven. When
cooked, remove the lamb, keeping the vegetables and potatoes on top, pour
off the sauce, reduce if needed and add one or two knobs of butter for a
rich texture. Taste this for seasoning, place the four chops onto some
plates and , if the potato has not coloured enough you may just lightly
brush with butter and put under the grill to give more of a golden colour.
Pour the sauce over and around and sprinkle with chopped parsley.

This dish is full of natural flavours from the vegetables, potato and meat
which have all been cooked in the sauce and are full of the lamb taste.
This is a wonderful, classic British dish.

Gary Rhodes
The Castle Hotel
Castle Green
Taunton
Somerset

Pork Roast with Honey and Garlic

Serves 6

32 oz pork fillet	2 tblsp soy sauce
3 cloves garlic	2 tblsp dry sherry
1 teasp salt	1 oz soft brown sugar
2" cube root ginger, peeled	2 tblsp sesame oil
2 tblsp clear honey	2-3 eating apples

Remove any fat or membrane from the pork and prick the flesh all over with a fork.
Prepare the marinade: cut the ginger into small pieces and place it into a food processor together with all the other ingredients except the honey. Liquidise to a pulp. Mix in the honey. Put all into a china dish and marinade for up to 6 hours, turning now and again.
To cook: let pork reach room temperature. Heat oven to Gas Mark 4. Roast pork on rack for 20 minutes basting occasionally.
While pork is cooking, puree apples together with some of the marinade, heat and serve as sauce for pork.
Serve sliced.

Bryan and Elizabeth Ferriss
Maiden Newton House
Maiden Newton
Nr Dorchester
Dorset

Boiled Gammon

15 lb piece of Gammon - boned and rolled
3 pints strong beer
1½ lb clear honey
1 large onion
1 whole celery
5 large carrots
2 leeks
1 fennel

Soak gammon overnight. Drain off the liquid. Roughly chop all vegetables and put in the saucepan with the gammon. Pour the beer and honey over the gammon. Then fill the saucepan with water until the gammon is covered. Bring to the boil and then cook for 3 hours. Leave gammon in the liquid to rest for approximately another 3 hours. Then remove gammon from the liquid and gently peel off the skin. The gammon can then be dressed e.g. breadcrumbs or just carved straight away.

Oliver Godfrey
Le Grandgousier
15 Western Street
Brighton
Sussex

Entrecote Montezuma

8 oz Entrecote steak per person, seasoned and cooked to required stage.
Spread top side of steak with 1 oz Montezuma paste and nappe with mixture
of semi-whipped cream and egg yolk. Put under high grill until cream has
melted and turned brown. Serve with red wine sauce around and sprinkle
with chopped parsley.

To Make Montezuma Paste

Finely dice red capsicum peppers, green capsicum pepper, onions and
cucumber. These are sweated off in a pan with olive oil, tomato puree
added, cook for five minutes, add red wine, simmer and reduce until paste
consistency. Remove from the heat and allow to cool. Add fresh parsley.

Karl Wadsack
The Three Lions
Stuckton
Fordingbridge
Hampshire

Steak and Guinness Pie

Serves 4

300g puff pastry	25g brown sugar
500g diced chuck steak	10g chopped parsley
100g sliced onion	50ml veal or beef stock
2 cloves garlic	seasoning
100ml Guinness	50ml oil
25g flour	

Heat a large pan with the oil. Season and flour the meat and brown in the
hot oil and remove from the pan. Reduce heat, add the onion and garlic and
cook slowly until soft and brown. Add the Guinness and brown sugar and
reduce by half. Return the meat back to the pan, add the stock and cook
slowly for 1 hour. Correct the seasoning, pour into a pie dish and allow
to cool. Roll out the pastry to 1/8 inch thickness and lay on the pie
dish. Brush with lightly beaten egg and bake in a medium oven for 30
minutes.

Clive Howe
The Lygon Arms
Broadway
Worcestershire

Coeur De Filet De Boeuf A La Daube

Prime fillet steak with baby vegetables and horseradish sauce

Serves 4

4 x 160g beef fillet
salt and freshly ground pepper
30g shallots
60g paysanne of vegetables
60g celery julienne
10cl red wine
2cl calvados
30cl beef consomme (double)
10g fresh horseradish
30g tarragon
30g diced tomatoes
60g butter to finish
30g grated horseradish (creamed)
30g chopped shallots
15g Pommery mustard
15g chopped parsley

Season and cook the beef fillets to taste, remove, dry and keep warm.
Saute some shallots in a little butter without colour and add the paysanne
of vegetables.
Season, remove, dry and keep warm.
Saute and season the celery and keep warm.
Deglace the cooking pan from the beef with the red wine and calvados.
Reduce by 1/3rd and add the double beef consomme and further reduce by
1/3rd.
Pass through a fine sieve and return to the stove.
Infuse the horseradish and tarragon and add the vegetables and tomatoes.
Mount with the butter and place the sauce upon the plate.
Mix the shallots, horseradish, parsley and mustard together and place upon
the steak.
Put the steak on the centre of the sauce and serve immediately.

Alan J Hill
The Gleneagles Hotel
Auchterarder
Perthshire
Scotland

Meat Sauce (Traditional Bolognese)

60 lb mince
16 lb chopped onions
4 lb celery
3½ lb chopped capsicum
2 oz mixed herbs
2 oz oregano
½ oz bay leaves
5 kg tomato puree
¼ gal Worcester sauce
2½ kg demiglace
2 ltr red wine
2 pints oil
1 lb sugar
4 oz salt
1 oz black pepper
4 oz beef boullion
2 oz garlic
18 pints water
3 tins chopped tomatoes
(gravy browning if needed)

Put oil, onions, herbs, garlic, Worcester sauce, sugar, capsicum, celery
and seasoning in a large pot.
Sweat off vegetables until tender.
Add mince and red wine, stirring out any lumps in the mince.
Cook out the mince (avoid over-cooking as it will begin to render down and
emit a lot of fat).
Add the chopped tomatoes, tomato puree and the stock. Add gravy browning
if needed.
Bring the sauce back to the boil stirring continuously, remove from the
heat soon after the sauce comes back to the boil. Ensure that the sauce is
put in storage containers as soon as possible and that these containers are
then put in the cold room after cooling for 2 hours.

N.B. SAUCES DO NOT NEED TO BE COLD BEFORE THEY ARE PUT IN THE COLD ROOM AND
SHOULD NEVER BE LEFT OUT OVERNIGHT.

Per portion:
        12 oz spaghetti
         7 oz meat sauce

Eamonn Hunter
Browns Restaurant
5,7,& 9 Woodstock Road
Oxford

110

Beef Wellington or Boeuf en Croute

Serves minimum of 4

2 lb whole fillet (trimmed of fat and gristle)
4 oz duxelles - see below
4 oz chicken liver pate (optional)
1 lb puff pastry

Place completely trimmed fillet in a pre-heated oven Gas mark 7, for 10 minutes (rare), 15 minutes (medium) or 25 minutes (well done). After desired cooking period remove from oven and allow to cool completely. Make Duxelles as follows:- 1 small onion, 1 clove garlic, 6 oz mushrooms, 1 oz butter, salt and pepper to taste. Thyme to add extra flavour, just a pinch. Chop all the Duxelles ingrdients finely and gently saute with the butter for about 30 minutes. You should have a firm but pliable mixture, allow to cool completely. Roll out pastry until big enough to entirely enclose the fillet of beef, from both of the largest sides of the fillet. Place the fillet in the centre of the rectangular piece of pastry. Place the cooled Duxelles and chicken liver pate over the top and then seal with a little egg wash. Cook for a further 20 minutes in a gas mark 7 oven and then allow to rest for 10 minutes.
Serve with a red wine or Bernaise sauce. French beans, calabrese and boiled new potatoes and excellent vegetables to accompany.

Adrian Clarke
The Fox and Goose
Fressingfield
Diss
Norfolk

Steak, Mushroom and Guinness Pie

80lb stewing steak
5 kg tomato puree
¼ gal Worcester sauce
2½ oz mixed herbs
½ oz bay leaves
1 lb sugar
6 pts Guinness
4 oz beef bouillon (mixed with 4 gal water)
16 lb onions
7 lb carrots
4 lb celery
8 lb mushrooms
4 oz salt
2 oz black pepper
2½ kg demiglace

Put the stewing steak, Guinness, herbs, sugar, seasoning and Worcester sauce in a large pot (12 gal). Cover the meat with stock, bring to the boil and simmer until the meat is tender, (approximately 2 hours). Add the vegetables and bring back to the boil, simmer until the vegetables are tender.
Add the tomato puree.
Mix the demiglace with ½ gallon water and add to the sauce. Bring back to the boil and season.

Ensure that the sauce is put in storage containers as soon as possible and that these containers are then put in the cold room after cooling for 2 hours.

N.B. SAUCES DO NOT NEED TO BE COLD BEFORE THEY ARE PUT IN THE COLD ROOM AND SHOULD NEVER BE LEFT OUT OVERNIGHT.

Per Portion:
          Cover with a plain pastry top. Serve on a plank and garnish
          with watercress.

Eamonn Hunter
Browns Restaurant
5,7,& 9 Woodstock Road
Oxford

Boeuf A La Mode

3½ - 4 lbs rump steak in a piece
2 - 3 large onions and about a dozen very small ones or
      shallots.
celery
garlic
bayleaf
black pepper
salt
oil
red wine

Place the piece of rump in a basin and pour over two or three tablespoons
of oil and red wine. Slice the large onions over this and a good
sprinkling of salt and pepper. Add bay leaf and garlic. Leave this to
marinade for 24 hours, turning occasionally. Take out the onion and fry in
butter till dark brown. Then fry the piece of meat on all sides, browning
thoroughly. Lift gently (without piercing) and put into casserole with
finely chopped celery, peeled small onions, seasonings and strained
marinade juice. Put firmly fitting lid on casserole and cook very, very
slowly for about four hours.

Therese Boswell
Combe House
Gittisham
Nr Honiton
Devon

Veal in Mustard and Grape Sauce

Serves 4

4 veal escalopes (approximately 6 oz each)
½ lb seedless grapes
1 large wine glass sweet sherry
1 pint double cream
1 tblsp English mustard
croutons for garnish

Mix sweet sherry, cream and mustard together in bowl.
In a little butter, start to fry the escalopes gently browning each side.
Add the mixture to the veal and bring to the boil. Then add the grapes -
reduce the liquid until a creamy mixture - then remove and serve.
Arrange escalopes on the serving dish and finally garnish with croutons.

Oliver Godfrey
Le Grandgousier
15 Western Street
Brighton
Sussex

Calf's Sweetbreads in Brioche with Grapes, marinated in Fino Sherry

Serves 6

24 hours in advance, blanche 1 lb sweetbreads, drain, press and chill,
Peel and seed 1 lb white grapes and soak in fino sherry.

Brioche

½ oz fresh yeast
8 oz strong plain flour
½ teaspoon salt
½ oz caster sugar
2 eggs
2 oz butter

Blend yeast with 2 teaspoons warm water. Sift flour, salt and sugar, then
add yeast liquid, eggs and cool soft butter. Work to soft dough. Knead
well and allow to prove in a warm place for one hour. Prepare 6 buttered
moulds and place ball of dough in each, only half filling mould. Allow to
rise again and bake in medium oven for 20 minutes to ½ hour. Turn out on
cake rack to cool.

Filling

½ pint chicken stock)
¼ pint white wine   ) reduce by half
2 oz butter

Slice sweetbreads evenly, add to liquid for 2 minutes then remove and keep
warm. Finish sauce by adding grapes and sherry, then add the butter in
small pieces until sauce is smooth.

To serve

Remove brioche tops and hollow out. Add sliced sweetbreads with some of
the sauce, pour remainder of sauce on plate around brioche and replace
tops.

Stephen and Penny Ross
Homewood Park Hotel
Hinton Charterhouse
Bath
Avon

Steak, Kidney and Mushroom Pie

Serves 4

600g topside of beef
60g beef kidney
salt and freshly ground pepper
2cl oil
30g butter
100g finely chopped onions
15g finely chopped garlic
100g button mushrooms
10cl white wine
60g tomato puree
40cl beef gravy
30g mixed chopped herbs
Worcester sauce
100g puff pastry
1 egg
30g chopped parsley

Season and seal the topside of beef in hot oil, remove and dry.
Do the same process for the beef kidneys and place it alongside the beef.
Place some butter in a pan and cook the onions and garlic with no colour,
add the mushrooms and deglace with the white wine.
Place the meat into the saucepan and bind together with the tomato puree.
Add the beef gravy and herbs, slightly seasoning with a touch of Worcester
sauce.
Cook for two hours until the meat is tender.
Once cooked, add the parsley and check the seasoning then place into the
serving bowl.
Top with the pastry and egg wash.
Cook in a hot oven until the pie crust is golden brown.
Serve immediately.

Alan J Hill
The Gleneagles Hotel
Auchterarder
Perthshire
Scotland

VEGETARIAN

Parsley Pie

Short Crust Pastry

4 oz flour
2 oz butter
1 teasp icing sugar
1 beaten egg (to mix)

Filling

½ lb chopped onions
3 oz butter
½ pint double cream
2 beaten eggs
salt and pepper
fine herbs: 3 - 4 tblsp chopped parsley
              1 tblsp chives
                 (dried or fresh)
              1 tblsp tarragon
1 tblsp watercress
2 finely chopped spring onions

Line fluted or plain flan tin, approximatly 9½ inches in diameter and with
a removable base, with short crust pastry.
Melt butter in a heavy pan and sweat onions until they are transparent.
Cool and beat cream, eggs and herb mixture together and season well. Add
onions and put into pastry case. Bake for about 40 minutes in a moderate
oven - Mark 3-4, 350deg - 375deg.
This tart can be eaten hot or cold but warm I think.

Francis Coulson and Brian Sack
Sharrow Bay Hotel
Lake Ullswater
Penrith
Cumbria

Gratin De Poireaux Au Roquefort

Gratin of leeks with Roquefort cheese

1 kg/2 lb 3 oz tender leeks
20g flour
100g/4oz Roquefort cheese, crumbled

20g butter
300ml/11 fl oz milk
salt and pepper

Cook the leeks in boiling salted water until soft, lift them out of the
water (reserve the water) and leave to drain in a warm place.
While the leeks are cooking, melt the butter in a saucepan, stir in the
flour and cook for 2 minutes to make a roux, add the milk and 200ml/7 fl oz
cooking water from the leeks and cook for 10 minutes, stirring
continuously. Add the Roquefort and cook for a further 5 minutes, then
check the seasoning.
Arrange the leeks in a gratin dish, pour over the sauce and brown the top
under a hot grill.

Pierre Koffmann
La Tante Claire
68/69 Royal Hospital Road
London

Spinach and Cheese Crouton Salad with Blue Cheese Dressing

1 lb fresh spinach (trimmed, stalked and roughly cut)
1 yellow pepper)
1 red pepper   ) cut into strips
3 thick slices wholemeal bread
5 oz cheddar cheese
2 oz walnuts

Prepare spinach and peppers.
Toast one side of bread, spread on garlic paste (if desired) and grated
cheese. Grill.
Cut into squares when cold.
Toss all ingredients together.

Blue Cheese Tofu Mayonnaise

EGGLESS!

3 oz blue cheese
10 oz Tofu
1 tsp sesame oil
2 tblsp rice vinegar
1 tsp dry mustard
salt, pepper and garlic
2 tsp lemon juice
¼ pint peanut or olive oil (or blend of the two)

Blend all ingredients, gently drizzling in the oil, to form a smooth thick
mayonnaise.

Jane Stimpson
Food For Thought
31 Neal Street
Covent Garden
London

Swiss Cheese Tart

Make a rich short-crust pastry case:

4 oz butter
6 oz flour
one egg
3 tblsp sugar
pinch salt

Cook blind, carefully.

Filling:
6 oz cream cheese
½ teacup cream
2 egg yolks
4 tblsp sugar
grating of lemon or orange rind
2 egg whites, beaten to a stiff froth

Pound cheese with cream, egg yolks, sugar and lemon rind, lastly add egg whites.
Spread mixture on the cooked pastry and put in moderate oven for 15 minutes.

Therese Boswell
Combe House
Gittisham
Near Honiton
Devon

Savoury Oat, Cheese and Onion Roast

This is a delicious savoury dish which we used to cook when I had a small cafe on the island -EVERYONE always asked for the recipe, and yet the ingredients are perfectly everyday and the method simple. It is good served hot with jacket potatoes, grilled tomatoes and mushrooms, or cold as a picnic dish with green salad and a good homemade coleslaw.

Serves 4

2 oz (50g) butter
1 lb (450g) onions, peeled and finely chopped
2 fat cloves garlic, peeled and crushed (optional)
2 teaspoons Marmite
8 oz (225g) porridge oats
6-8oz (175-225g) Cheddar cheese, grated
1-2 tablespoons finely chopped mixed fresh herbs OR
2-3 teaspoons mixed dried herbs
2 large eggs, lightly beaten
pinch of salt
freshly ground black pepper

Pre-heat the oven to gas mark 5, 375F (190C).

In a very large heavy frying pan, melt the butter and gently fry the onions and garlic (if using), stirring them around occasionally, until they are soft and transparent, but do not allow them to brown. Stir in the Marmite and allow it to melt into the onions. Now tip the onions into a large mixing bowl and stir in the porridge oats, grated cheese and herbs, mixing well with a large spoon. Add the eggs and season the mixture to taste with salt and pepper. The mixture should be stiffish and of a dropping consistency.

Turn into a lightly buttered 8-9 inch (20-23cm) baking dish or deep flan dish and bake in the oven for about 40 minutes or until firm and golden brown on top. To serve, slice into wedges at the table.

NB. For a lighter version, separate the eggs. Add the beaten yolks to the mixture, as above. Whisk the whites until stiff, and carefully fold into the mixture, and bake as above.

Susan Hicks. After her very successful BBC TV series and accompanying book The Fish Course, Susan has now written The Main Course. She lives on The Isles of Scilly.

Arame and Alfalfa Salad with Sesame and Orange Dressing

Serves 6

½ oz Arame seaweed (cover with hot water and a little Tamari. Leave for 5 minutes then drain.)

2 oz Alfalfa
4 oz smoked Tofu (cut into small squares)
½ red pepper (finely chopped)
3 spring onions (finely chopped)
1 oz parsley (finely chopped)
1 orange split into segments

Dressing:

1 dessertsp sesame oil	½ dessertsp Tamari
1 dessertsp rice vinegar	1 dessertsp sugar
3 dessertsp orange juice	½ dessertsp lemon juice
1 dessertsp olive oil	pepper and salt

Combine. Put into a screw top jar and shake.

Jane Stimpson
Food for Thought
31 Neal Street
Covent Garden
London

120

PUDDINGS

White Chocolate Mousse encased in Tuille Wafers

Serves 8

Chocolate Mousse:
300g white chocolate (melt in bain marie)
2 egg yolks   )
3 dessertspoons icing sugar) Sabayon
brandy and pistachio paste to taste
¾ litre double cream (semi whipped)

Pear Sorbet:
1 pint stock syrup
juice of ½ lemon
8 Conference pears
100g glucose

Tuille Wafers:
110g caster sugar
130g plain flour
150g butter
150g egg white

Cream all dry ingredients together and finally bind with egg white.

Chocolate Mousse:
Whisk eggs and sugar until amalgamated.
Melt the chocolate in bain marie.
Add chocolate to the egg mixture and mix vigourously.
Add brandy and pistachio paste to taste - this will bring the mousse back
to a smooth texture.
Finally fold in the semi whipped cream - NB do not overmix, it may split
the mousse.

An assortment of fruit garni at base of plate, on a fruit coulis. Between
two pear shaped wafers pipe enough mousse. Sprinkle chopped pistachio nuts
and assemble together. Pipe dark chocolate onto the leaf of the top wafer.
Dust with icing sugar and place on top of a rosette of mousse at a 15
degree angle from fruit garni.
To the left, garnish with 2 teaspoon quenelles of pear sorbet facing away
from the pear stalk.
Garnish with a small mint leaf.

Nigel Haworth
Northcote Manor
Northcote Road
Langho
Blackburn
Lancashire

Chocolate Mousse

8 oz dark chocolate
¾ pint double cream
5 eggs
3 oz caster sugar

Melt the chocolate gently beforehand. In a metal bowl put the 3 oz sugar,
3 whole eggs and two egg yolks, please keep the two whites. Over a pan of
boiling water, beat the eggs and sugar until thick, quite hot and creamy,
taking care not to scramble the eggs, you will know when the mixture is
ready because the whisk will leave a trail if lifted out. Now cool the
eggs and sugar, either by putting it in a machine and beating until cold,
or by beating it in a bowl on ice cold water. The mixture should be quite
cold, pale in colour and quite thick. Beat the egg whites until thick and
frothy, slowly add the melted chocolate to the eggs and sugar, mixing
thoroughly to avoid chocolate chips, then fold in the egg whites. At this
stage a small amount of alcohol can be added, e.g. cointreau or rum. Put
the mixture either into a large bowl or several small ramekins to set,
which should take 2-3 hours. Before serving, decorate with orange
segments.

Sonya Kidney
The Marsh Goose
Moreton in Marsh
Gloucestershire

Strawberry Mousse

1 lb strawberries
3 dessertspoons sugar
4 leaves of gelatine
3 egg whites
1 pint double cream

Prepare the strawberries and puree in the liquidiser. Sieve, preferably
through muslin, until the seeds have been removed. Add two dessertspoons
sugar, more if you prefer. Soak the leaves of gelatine in a little water
until soft then gently dissolve in a little strawberry liquor or puree over
a low heat.

Beat the egg whites with a tablespoon of sugar. Whisk the gelatine into
the puree then fold in the lightly whipped cream and the egg whites. Pour
into moulds. Allow to set in the fridge.
To turn out, dip the moulds briefly into warm water and turn onto serving
plates. Surround with strawberry sauce and fresh strawberries.

Stephen Smith
The Belvedere Hotel
19 North Park Road
Bradford
West Yorkshire

Chocolate Mousse Basque

6 oz plain block chocolate
2-3 tablespoons water, or black coffee
½ oz butter
1 dessertspoon brandy
3 eggs

Break the chocolate into small pieces, put into a pan with the liquid and stir continually over a gentle heat to a thick cream. The chocolate should be hot but the sides of the pan never so hot that you cannot touch them. Take off the heat, stir in the butter and flavouring.

Crack each of the eggs, putting the whites into a basin and dropping the yolks, one at a time, into the chocolate pan; stir well after each addition.
Watchpoint: It is important that the chocolate is hot when the yolks go in so that they get slightly cooked.

Whisk the whites to a firm snow, then stir briskly into the chocolate. When thoroughly mixed fill the small pots and leave overnight in the larder or refrigerator.

For easy pouring turn the mixture first into a jug, scraping the pan out well.

Oliver Godfrey
Le Grandgousier
15 Western Street
Brighton
Sussex

Mango Mousse

½ lb mango flesh
2 egg yolks and whites
2 leaves gelatine
2 oz sugar
lemon juice

Scoop out the flesh, puree and sieve. Add the lemon juice. Beat the egg yolks with sugar until pale. Soften the gelatine in a little water then add to the mango puree and heat gently until the gelatine has dissolved. Cool until it begins to thicken then add to the egg yolks, fold in the lightly whipped cream and the stiffly whisked egg whites. Pour into moulds and allow to set. Turn out and surround with the sauce of your choice, for example passion fruit or orange.

Stephen Smith
The Belvedere Hotel
19 North Park Road
Bradford
West Yorkshire

Cinnamon Souffle with Drambuie Cream

Serves 4

1 lb 6 oz pears
1 pint water
1 level teasp cornflour
1 level tablesp water
3 level tablesp cinnamon
3 oz sugar
5 egg whites
½ pint whipping cream
½ oz sugar
½ measure Drambuie
Note: Any fruit may be used with the same method but, obviously, leave out the cinnamon.

For the panade:
Roughly chop the pears.
Place in saucepan, barely cover with water and cook until soft.
Liquidise and pass through a sieve. Place back onto stove in clean pan.
Simmer until thick, stirring occasionally (approximately 10 minutes)
Mix the cornflour and water together. Whisk into pear mixture and leave on a low heat for approximately 10 minutes.
Add cinnamon powder and whisk.

Note: This mixture can be used immediately or kept in the fridge for later use.

For the cream:
Whisk the cream until it peaks. Add sugar and Drambuie to taste.

Making the Souffle:
Warm the panade gently in a bain marie.
Whisk egg whites in a copper bowl until they peak. Add sugar a little at a time.
Mix a spoon of whites into panade, then fold in the rest.
Butter and sugar ramekin moulds.
Spoon in souffle mixture until 1" above the rim. Smooth off around the edge at a 35 degree angle with a palette knife, finishing with a flat top.
Place on a baking sheet in a pre-heated oven at a gas mark 7 for approximately 10-12 minutes.
Serve dusted with icing sugar and a saucer of cream - IMMEDIATELY.

Chris Oakes
Oakes Restaurant
169 Slad Road
Stroud
Gloucestershire

Iced Almond Souffle

Serves 4

1 whole egg
1 egg yolk
50 g sugar
1 measure of Almond liqueur (or almond essence)
5 fl oz cream (whipped)
cocoa powder

Whisk the egg and egg yolk and sugar together in a bowl over a pan of hot water until thick, light and frothy.
Remove from heat and place in mixing bowl and beat for 10 minutes.
Fold in whipped cream and add liqueur.
Pour into four large ramekin dishes and freeze.
To serve dust with cocoa powder

John Mann
The Montagu Arms Hotel at Beaulieu
Palace Lane
Beaulieu
Hampshire

Iced Cointreau Souffle

Serves 6 - 8

3 egg whites
3 oz caster sugar
¼ pint whipping cream
1 egg yolk
1 drop vanilla essence
2 measures Cointreau

Whisk egg whites and half the sugar until thick.
Whisk cream.
Add egg yolks, remaining sugar, vanilla essence and Cointreau to the cream stirring gently with a wooden spoon.
Fold together with the egg whites and put into individual dishes.
Freeze for 6-8 hours.

These can be served straight from the freezer, decorated with whipped cream and a few flaked almonds.

Sue and Barry Davies
Salisbury House
84 Victoria Road
Diss
Norfolk

Chocolate and Orange Souffle

Serves 4

2 oz butter
2 oz plain flour
½ pint milk
3 egg yolks
4 egg whites
4 oz sugar
3 oz dark chocolate
zest of one orange

Melt chocolate and milk together and put aside.
In a thick bottomed pan melt the butter, stir in the flour and cook and
stir for one minute, being careful not to burn it, pour in all the milk and
beat until the mixture starts to leave the side of the pan. Remove from
heat, beat in the sugar first, then the egg yolks and finally the orange
zest.

This can be made in advance.

To cook:

Beat egg whites stiffly then fold carefully into the rest of the mixture.
It does not have to be fully smooth.

Pour into a buttered and sugared 2 pint souffle dish, it should be about
2/3 up the dish, and bake in a hot oven, approximately 20 minutes or until
well risen, could also be put into individual souffle dishes, will take
approximately 10-12 minutes to cook.

Stephen and Anne Frost
The Stonor Arms
Stonor
Nr Henley-on-Thames
Oxfordshire

Hazelnut Praline Souffle

Serves 20

Base:

3 cups milk
9 tablsp caster sugar
¾ cup flour
18 egg yolks
18 egg whites

Praline:

1 cup sugar
¼ cup water
cream of tartare
1 cup hazelnuts

Caramelize the above sugar and water.
Add the hazelnuts - which have been blended well.
Turn out onto oiled surface or buttered foil.

Butter ramekins twice then line with caster sugar.
Simmer milk.
Mix sugar, flour, and yolks well.
Pour over milk and simmer stirring continuously.
Thicken.
Strain, cover and cool.
Whisk egg whites until stiff.
Add 4 tablsp. sugar.
Mix praline into custard and fold in whites carefully.
Fill ramekins and sprinkle with fine praline.
Bake at 400 deg for 13 minutes (middle of oven).
Serve immediately.

Colin John Bussey
The Gleneagles Hotel
Auchterarder
Perthshire

Hot Passion Fruit Souffle

Serves 1 or 2

2 egg yolks
2 egg whites
2 oz passion fruit juice
1 oz sugar
½ teaspoon passion fruit zest

Butter and sugar souffle moulds.
Whisk egg yolks with sugar over heat.
Add passion fruit juice and zest and whisk together well.
Fold in whisked egg whites and ¾ fill moulds.
Bake at 200 deg C for 10 minutes.
Serve at once as it will fall quickly.

Nick Buckingham
Cavendish Hotel
Baslow
Derbyshire

Bramley Apple and Honey Souffle

2 lbs apples
2 oz brown sugar
juice of lemon
4 oz water
2 oz butter
1½ oz cornflour (in paste form)
½ pint of egg white
Honey to taste.

Cut apples into small pieces and discard cores.
Melt the butter and brown sugar in a saucepan and add the apples. Stir
this into the butter and pour in the lemon juice and water. Place a lid on
the saucepan and continue to cook out over a moderate heat until the apples
are cooked and most of the moisture has gone. Now liquidise and pass the
pulp through a sieve and return to a clean saucepan. Reduce the pulp
further and add the honey. Whisk in the cornflour paste until a dropping
consistency has been reached. Ensure mixture is cooked out and then pour
into a clean bowl to cool.

Whisk the egg whites until peak then add a sprinkling of sugar to smooth
out the whites. When they are of a reasonably stiff consistency remove
from the machine. Spoon half the whites into the apple mix and whisk
together.

The remaining half must be folded in thoroughly to give lightness. Place
mixture into buttered and sugared ramekins and bake for 7-8 minutes at gas
mark 6.

Ramon Farthing
Calcot Manor
Near Tetbury
Gloucestershire

Mango Ice Cream with Brandy Snap and Juice of Passion Fruit

4 egg yolks
4 ripe large mangoes (1 lb of flesh required)
6 oz caster sugar
½ pint lightly whipped cream
juice of one lemon
½ pint milk

Make a custard by whisking the yolks and sugar together, pouring on the hot milk, return to a clean pan and cook gently until thickened. Allow to cool.

Cut the mangoes in half lengthways, twist to open, scoop out the flesh, catching the juice in a bowl, scrape off the flesh from the stones, puree in a liquidiser and sieve. Add to the cold custard, stir in the lemon juice and fold in the lightly whipped cream. Freeze.

To make the sauce, bring one pint of water and half a pound of sugar to the boil. Wash eight passion fruits, cut in half, scoop out the centre into a sieve over a bowl to catch the juice. Place the shells in the syrup and simmer until the flavour has been released into the syrup. Add the collected passion fruit pips and simmer for two minutes. Strain and pour in the juice. Bring to the boil and skim. Allow to cool.

Serve the ice cream in a brandy snap cup with the sauce spooned over the ice cream and around the plate. Decorate with diced mango.

For the brandy snap cup: mix together to a smooth paste one tablespoon of golden syrup, two ounces of butter, two ounces of plain flour and one tablespoon of brandy. Lightly grease a baking sheet with butter and place approximately ¾ inch round spoonfuls of mixture well spaced at regular intervals on the tray. Cook in a hot oven until golden brown. Allow to cool only slightly and remove with a palette knife and shape on the back of dariole mould or a teacup. When cold store in airtight containers. If left out they will go soft very quickly, especially if there is a lot of moisture in the kitchen. If you find difficulty in removing the brandy snap from the tray use parchment paper.

Stephen Smith
The Belvedere Hotel
19 North Park Road
Bradford
West Yorkshire

Pear Ice Cream

4 egg yolks
8 oz caster sugar
½ pint milk
4 ripe pears
1 pint whipped cream

Beat the egg yolks and sugar until pale. Heat the milk and pour onto the egg yolks. Return to a clean pan and cook gently until it begins to thicken. Allow this mixture to go completely cold. Peel and core the pears. Liquidise them and mix into the cold custard mixture. Fold in the whipped cream. Pour into the ice-cream maker and freeze. The addition of chopped stem ginger and ginger syrup to the ice cream is a perfect match. The ice cream can be served with an Almond Tuile with Mango Sauce.

Stephen Smith
The Belvedere Hotel
19 North Park Road
Bradford
West Yorkshire

Figs poached in Red Wine, with Fig and Cinnamon Ice Cream

12 fresh ripe purple figs
½ pint red wine
½ pint water
¾ lb sugar
3 egg yolks
6 fl oz milk
1 cinnamon stick
2 oz caster sugar
6 fl oz whipping cream

Combine the wine, water and ¾ lb sugar and bring to the boil in a pan, add the figs and simmer gently for a few minutes. Allow to cool. Puree and sieve six of the figs and set aside. Whisk the egg yolks and 2 oz of sugar until pale, heat the milk in a pan with the cinnamon stick, pour on to the egg yolks, return to a clean pan, stir until the mixture begins to thicken, pour into a bowl and allow to cool completely.

Remove the cinnamon stick and add the pureed figs. Whisk the cream and fold into the mixture. Pour into the ice cream machine and freeze. Serve with the remaining figs.

Stephen Smith
The Belvedere Hotel
19 North Park Road
Bradford
West Yorkshire

Port and Claret Jelly

¾ pint (400ml) cold water
8 oz (225g) cube sugar
2 tablespoons redcurrant jelly
half stick of cinnamon
¾ pint (400ml) claret
½ pint (300ml) port
2 tablesp brandy
just under 1 oz (25g) powdered gelatine

This is a light, tipsy-like dessert, requiring little or no effort of digestion. Served in silver goblets on a doyleyed plate with a head of a seasonal flower (not too scented, mind you) and a piece of shortbread, you have a simple, but quite divine ending to your meal.

In one clean saucepan put the cold water with the cube sugar along with the redcurrant jelly and cinnamon. Bring to the boil.
In a second clean saucepan, pour the claret, port and brandy. (The claret doesn't have to be Chateau Haut Brion Pessac 1966 or the Port, Taylors 1960. Rough Vin Rouge from Bordeaux will suffice and so will Taylors Mesquita Port, and Napoleon Cooking Brandy is fine.) On top of the alcohol mixture as it comes to the boil sprinkle just under 1 oz (25g) of Davies's gelatine. Then leave both pans simmering for 10 minutes.
Pass the contents of both pans through a fine sieve into a large jug, stir swiftly and as it is cooling, pour into dishes or goblets. These quantities make 12 adequate portions (don't forget the jelly is rather intoxicating so don't give enormous helpings, and you don't have to serve dessert wine with the sweet, or probably even offer a liqueur!)
This recipe can be easily adapted to the tipple of your choice provided you do not stray from the actual quantities. In the winter Ginger Wine Jelly is rather pleasant (make up your mixture from Crabbies Green Ginger to the strength you personally like), and this particular jelly is rather nice if you put a spoonful of home-made mincemeat in the base.
Campari and Orange is quite nice but I forbid Gin and Lime at Miller Howe as on one occasion the cook put ¾ pint (400ml) gin to half a pint of lime juice and the result wasn't funny at all!

Biscuits to Accompany Jellies and Cream Ices

4 oz (100g) butter
4 oz (100g) sieved plain flour

4 oz (100g) caster sugar
4 egg whites, stiffly beaten

Cream together the butter and sugar and fold in the sieved flour. Then fold in the stiffly beated egg whites. Using a ¼ inch (5mm) plain nozzle, pipe the mixture onto oiled baking trays, covered with greaseproof paper. This mixture makes 48 biscuits, approximately 2½ inches (6cm) long. Bake at 375F, (190C) gas 5 for 15-20 minutes.

John Tovey
Miller Howe Hotel
Windermere
English Lakes

132

Lemon Cheesesake

Base:- 4 oz digestive biscuits
      2 oz melted butter
      1 oz caster sugar

8 oz 'Philly' cream cheese
2 egg yolks
4 oz sugar
8 fl oz double cream
2 leaves gelatine
2 egg whites
juice of 1 lemon

Pound biscuits with sugar until fine and then stir in the melted butter.
Line spring mould or cake tin with cling film and cover base with half of
biscuit mixture.
Beat together 'Philly', yolk and sugar until creamy.
In the meantime soak gelatine in cold water and squeeze of lemon.
Beat 2/3 rds of double cream to peak and then egg whites, also to peak.
Add remaining 1/3 rd double cream to cheese and beat once more, being
careful not to curdle the mixture.
Place lemon juice in a small saucepan, add 'squeezed' gelatine and melt
over gentle heat.
Add gelatine and lemon juice to mixture.
Fold in whipped cream, followed by the beaten whites.
Pour into mould and finally pour over remaining biscuits.
Allow to set for approximately 3 to 4 hours.

C E Oakley
The Pier At Harwich
The Quay
Harwich
Essex

Quick Lemon Cheesecake

This is a very quick cheesecake and good to make in hot weather as there's
no cooking involved.

Serves 6-8

For the base:
10 plain digestive biscuits (crushed to crumbs)
2½ oz butter (60g)
1 teaspoon soft brown sugar

For the filling:
12 oz cottage cheese (350g)
2½ oz caster sugar (60g)
the grated rind and juice of 2 lemons
2 size 1 egg yolks

½ oz powdered gelatine (10g)
¼ pint double cream (150ml)

You will also need an 8 inch (20cm) flan tin or sponge tin with a loose
base, lightly oiled.
First prepare the base by melting the butter in a small saucepan, then
combining it with the biscuit crumbs and sugar. Spoon the crumb mixture
into the prepared tin and press it well down all over as evenly as
possible. Now put the gelatine, along with 3 tablespoons of cold water,
into a small cup and stand this in a small saucepan of barely simmering
water. Leave it for about 10 minutes or until the gelatine looks clear and
transparent. Then remove it from the heat and leave it on one side.

Now put the egg yolks, sugar and cheese in a liquidiser, blend for about
one minute, then add the lemon juice and rind and the gelatine poured
through a strainer. Blend again until everything is thoroughly mixed and
the mixture absolutely smooth. Next, in a basin, whip the double cream
till 'floppy'; add that to the liquidiser and blend again for just a few
seconds. Now pour the mixture on to the biscuit base, cover with foil and
chill thoroughly for a least 3 hours. Before serving you can, if you wish,
add a few thin slices of lemon to decorate.

Delia Smith

Grape Cheesecake

Melt 100g butter and stir in 200g crushed digestive biscuits. Use to line
base of 20cm springclip cake tin.

Liquidise and sieve 480g white grapes.
Dissolve 11g gelatine in 6 tblsp of this juice.
In a mixing bowl beat 3 egg yolks to a ribbon consistency.
Add 225g cream cheese and 50g caster sugar and beat again.
Fold in 150ml double cream, lightly whipped, the remaining white grape
juice and gelatine, and place in 'fridge until on the point of setting.

Whisk 3 egg whites stiffly and fold in to mixture. Put back in the 'fridge
to set.

Liquidise 480g black grapes and sieve to use as an accompanying sauce.

Deseed 120g black grapes to use for decoration.

Joy Hadley
Rumbles Cottage Restaurant
Braintree Road
Felstead
Essex

Chocolate Coffee Pot with Tia Maria

1 lb dark chocolate
5 egg yolks
8 egg whites
2 dessertspoons caster sugar
5 heaped tsps. coffee
2½ fl oz water
2 fl oz Tia Maria
5 fl oz double or whipping cream

Dissolve the coffee in hot water and add to the Tia Maria. Place the broken chocolate and egg yolks in a bowl and add the liquid. Stir gently over a pan of hot water until melted. Do not overheat otherwise the yolks will scramble. Allow to cool then fold in the cream, whisk the egg whites until light and fluffy, add the sugar then fold carefully a little at a time into the chocolate. Pour into ramekins and allow to set overnight if possible in the fridge.

Chocolate Orange Trifle

6 egg yolks
4 oz caster sugar
1 oz cocoa powder
¾ oz flour
¾ oz cornflour
pint of milk
¼ pint double cream plus 1 pint for the top
¾ to 1 lb fatless chocolate sponge
chocolate mousse (using the Chocolate Pot recipe but omit the coffee and water and substitute Cointreau for Tia Maria plus 2½ fl oz of milk)
orange segments from two oranges

To make the custard bring the milk to the boil with half the sugar. Whisk the remaining sugar and egg yolks until the mixture becomes pale, combine the flours and cocoa powder and whisk into the yolk mixture. Heat the milk and pour on to the mixture and return to a clean wet pan and cook through for two or three minutes over a moderate heat, whisking continuously.

Turn the custard into a bowl and cover with cling-film to prevent a skin forming. When cool, fold in the lightly-whisked cream, cut the sponge into squares and sandwich together with the mousse, arrange in a suitable dish and sprinkle with Cointreau according to taste and some orange segments. Cover with the custard and allow to set; whip one pint of double cream and cover the top.

Stephen Smith
The Belvedere Hotel
19 North Park Road
Bradford
West Yorkshire

Apple Tart with Apple Sorbet

Entertaining friends to good food and wine is one of my loves. But having to cook for maybe six or eight people can be an awesome task and you will often find yourself having no time to enjoy the party. Well, the secret of good cooking is simplicity and so here I have a recipe for a delicious Apple Tart served with an Apple Sorbet. This dish can be made in advance so you won't have to worry about your dessert burning or melting! Firstly, buy good crisp Granny Smith apples which cook very nicely without breaking up and they also have a lovely sharp, tangy taste. You will need about 16 apples, 2 for each tart and 8 for the sorbet. If you don't have time to make puff pastry (most good cook books will have a recipe), buy frozen and for 4 people you will need about 8 oz.

Apple Sorbet
1 pint of water
1 lb sugar
8 Granny Smith apples

Mix the water with the sugar and bring to the boil. Boil for a few minutes. Peel, core and roughly chop the apples and place in a pan, just covering with some of the stock. Bring this to the simmer and, once the apples are cooked, puree in a liquidiser or push through a sieve. Place the mixture into a sorbet machine (if you don't have one, spread the puree onto a tray and place in the freezer. When at setting point whisk and do this several times until it has completely frozen). When the sorbet is made leave in the freezer. This can be made the day before.

Apple Tart
8 oz puff pastry
8 Granny Smith apples
butter
caster sugar
apricot jam

Roll out the pastry very thinly and leave to rest. Cut out 4 rounds of pastry (approximately 8" diameter) and place on baking trays. Peel, quarter and then slice apples. Place the slices onto the pastry, overlapping all the way around until the pastry is totally covered. Put a few knobs of butter onto the tart and sprinkle with a little caster sugar. Bake in a preheated oven (gas mark 7, 220 deg C, 425 deg F) for 10-15 minutes until the pastry is crisp and the apples start to colour.
The tart can be made in the morning and then, when you've finished your main course, it can be put back into the oven to warm.
To serve
Take tart from oven and lightly brush with hot apricot jam and put onto warm plates. Shape the sorbet between two tablespoons into a lozenge and, for colour, take a slice of green apple and place on top.

Gary Rhodes
The Castle Hotel
Castle Green
Taunton
Somerset

136

Gratin of Pear and Summer Berries presented on a Mint Anglais edged with Pear and Strawberry Coulis

Serves 4

Poire Eau de Vie to taste
2 Commice pears poached in stock syrup
1 lb strawberries
8 oz raspberries

Italian meringue:- 6 oz sugar
2 egg whites

Pastry cream:- ½ pint milk
1 oz flour
2 oz sugar
2 whole eggs
1 yolk

Shortbread biscuit:- 6 oz plain flour
4 oz butter
2 oz sugar

Mint Anglaise:- ½ pint milk
3 egg yolks
2 oz sugar
Fresh mint

Prepare the shortbread by rubbing the butter and flour together until a bread crumb, then carefully mix in the sugar and knead to a dough. Allow to rest for 30 minutes.

Roll out pastry very thin 1/8 inch then bake off in an oven at 325 for 8-10 minutes or until cooked. Do not brown. Remove from the oven and whilst still hot place 4 ring cutters on top and cut 4 circles. Leave in place until cold.

Prepare pastry cream by whisking whole egg, egg yolk, flour and sugar together use a little milk if needed. Boil the remainder of the milk and add to egg mixture. Mix then return to the heat and whisk until it thickens by boiling. When it is cooked it should be very thick. Remove and allow to cool.

Prepare mint anglaise by whisking egg yolks and sugar together. Boil milk with the mint and add to egg mixture. Return to the stove and slowly cook until it coats the back of a wooden spoon. DO NOT BOIL or it will separate. When cooked remove from the pan to prevent it cooking any more. Allow to cool then strain out the mint.

Prepare the meringue by mixing the sugar with a little water then slowly dissolve over heat then carefully raise the heat to 121F. As the temperature reaches 121F, using a electric whisk whip the 2 egg whites up, then carefully add the sugar syrup, continue to whisk until cold. Reserve for use.

When the pastry cream is cold, dice up one pear and macerate with a little
Eau de Vie, to this add ½ the strawberries which should be cut into pieces
the size of the pear, reserve 4 raspberries and add the rest to the
mixture. To this add 2 - 3 tablespoons of the pastry cream and mix
carefully.

With the remaining pear and strawberries, liquidise with a little stock
syrup and strain through a fine sieve.

Place the shortbread as a base in each of the 4 rings, then almost fill
with the fruit mixture, press down firmly then top with the meringue.
Carefully glaze with a gas blow lamp. or under a very hot grill.

Place the rings in the centre of 4 serving plates, surround with the mint
anglaise followed by the coulis. Blend these two together with a cocktail
stick to give a sun burst effect. Carefully remove the rings and decorate
with the reserved raspberries.

Bruce R Sangster
The Murrayshall
Country House Hotel and Restaurant
Scone
Perthshire

Ambrosia

Originates from Southern States of America

3 large oranges
1 small pineapple
2 oz caster sugar
5 oz desiccated coconut, soaked in
4 oz water for 30 minutes, then drained

Peel oranges, removing all pith and skin, cut into slices. Peel, core and
slice pineapple. Cut each slice into eight pieces. Combine the sugar and
coconut.

In your serving glasses, arrange fruit alternately in layers, sprinkling
each layer with a little of the coconut and sugar mixture. Chill for at
least two hours before serving. For a final touch, add a drop or two of
Kirsch!

Karl Wadsack
The Three Lions
Stuckton
Fordingbridge
Hampshire

Petit Pots de Chocolat

Serves 8

1 lb plain chocolate
2 tablesp water
10 eggs, separated
2 grated orange rind
5 oz caster sugar
fresh orange segments

Place chocolate and water in a mixing bowl and melt over a bain-marie.
Remove from heat and beat in the egg yolks one at a time.
Stir in the orange rind.
In a mixing machine whisk the egg whites and add the sugar gradually.
Mix all ingredients together and leave to set in the fridge.
When required pipe into serving dishes and decorate with fresh orange
segments and serve with some sweet biscuits.

Sweet Biscuits

2½ oz icing sugar
½ lb plain flour
½ lb butter
½ egg

Cream the sugar and butter.
Add the egg and then fold in the flour
Pipe onto a tray with silicone paper (shapes to your liking) and bake (gas
5-6) for 8 - 10 minutes.

Serve cold on a doilied plate, dust the biscuits with a little sieved icing
sugar.

N.B. This recipe for the chocolate pots is very rich and, therefore, only a
small portion should be served.

Robert Elsmore
Hunstrete House
Hunstrete
Chelwood
Near Bristol
Avon

Treacle Tart

1 finely chopped apple
zest and juice of ½ lemon
5 eggs
3¾ oz white breadcrumbs
¾ pint golden syrup
1/3rd pint double cream

Line a 10 in flan dish with sweet pastry and leave to rest for 45 minutes.
Mix together all the ingredients and pour into the flan dish. Cook at gas
5 or 190C until set. Serve warm with cream.

Stephen Smith
The Belvedere Hotel
19 North Park Road
Bradford
West Yorkshire

A Traditional English Steamed Pudding with Orange Custard

4 oz caster sugar
4 oz self-raising flour
3½ oz suet
¾ teaspoon mixed spice
zest of half a lemon and orange
one chopped apple
4 oz currants
two pieces of finely chopped stem ginger
3 eggs
black treacle

Mix all the dry ingredients together, then add the beaten eggs and one
tablespoon of black treacle. Pour into eight individual or one large
pudding basin 'lined' with golden syrup. Cover with greaseproof paper, tie
with string and steam for 35 minutes or one hour if using a large basin.

Orange Custard

Beat six egg yolks and 3 oz caster sugar until pale in colour. Pour on 1
pint hot milk stirring to blend together. Return to a clean wet pan and
gently cook until the custard thickens. Add the juice and zest of one
orange. Be careful not to overheat otherwise the custard will curdle.

Stephen Smith
The Belvedere Hotel
19 North Park Road
Bradford
West Yorkshire

Creme Brulee

1 pint double cream
6 egg yolks
2 oz sugar
1 split vanilla pod

Bring cream to the boil with the vanilla.
Whisk onto egg yolks and sugar.
Return mixture to cream pan and place into a hot water bath.
Over a gentle heat, stir continuously until the mixture begins to thicken.
Strain into individual ramekins or into one large serving dish. Allow to cool.
When cool, sieve brown sugar over the surface of the custard to form an even layer barely 1/8 inch thick.
Place under a hot grill to melt sugar, being careful not to burn it.
Cool again. then serve.

(place raspberries into each dish before adding custard as a delicious alternative.)

T J Brooks
Table Restaurant
135 Babbacombe Road
Babbacombe
Devon

Bread and Butter Pudding

6 eggs	currants
1 pint milk	sultanas
¾ pint cream	cherries
3 oz caster sugar	candied peel
demerara sugar	nutmeg
bread	

Slice the bread and remove the crusts. Butter each side. Cover the base of a greased oven-proof dish with some of the bread. Sprinkle with brown sugar and the fruit. Cover with another layer of bread and repeat the process. I usually have three layers. Beat the eggs with the milk, cream and sugar. Add some freshly-grated nutmeg and pour over the bread and fruit. Leave to stand for about 1½ hours. Cook in a bain-marie at gas 5 until set. Serve with pouring cream. Home-made bread or brioche makes a better pudding.

Stephen Smith
The Belvedere Hotel
19 North Park Road
Bradford
West Yorkshire

Ginger and Orange Syllabub

Serves 4-6

½ pint double cream
4 tablespoons dry sherry
1 tablespoon orange liqueur
1½ oz caster sugar
finely grated rind of 1 orange
2 pieces of finely chopped stem ginger
1 tablespoon ginger syrup

Place the ingredients in a deep bowl and whisk until the cream stands in soft peaks. Spoon into four or six tall glasses and chill until ready to serve. Decorate with whipped cream, orange segments and a chocolate decoration.

Stephen Smith
The Belvedere Hotel
19 North Park Road
Bradford
West Yorkshire

Strawberry Syllabub

1 lb fresh strawberries
¾ pint double cream
8 egg whites
8 oz sugar
lemon juice

Liquidise strawberries and add a few drops of lemon juice. Whip up egg whites until stiff - then add sugar slowly. In a separate bowl whip up the double cream until thick. Add cream to egg white mixture and also add the liquidised strawberries - fold all ingredients together.

Put mixture into ramekins.

Oliver Godfrey
Le Grandgousier
15 Western Street
Brighton
Sussex

Fraises A La Mataise

A good strawberry sweet after a rather rich main course.

Hull the strawberries , steep overnight in a bowl with the strained juice
of an orange and liquor glassful of curacao and icing sugar to taste.

Therese Boswell
Combe House
Gittisham
Near Honiton
Devon

Sticky Toffee Pudding

1¼ lb dates - stoned and chopped
1½ lb plain flour
8 oz butter
¾ lb demerara sugar
¼ lb soft brown sugar
3 tsp bicarbonate of soda
1½ pints boiling water
3 eggs
1 small tsp vanilla essence

Cream butter and sugar.
Add eggs and vanilla essence.
Put chopped dates in a bowl, coat in flour, add boiling water.
Add date mixture to butter and sugar.
Add flour and bicarbonate slowly.
Mix well.

Put into small 4" or 5" flan tins (makes 15 puddings in 4" tins)
Cook at 350 degrees F. for 20 - 30 minutes.

Sticky Toffee Sauce

Boil together:

8 oz butter
2 oz soft brown sugar
1 lb demerara sugar
3 fl oz cream

Raymond A Sharp
Kirkby Fleetham Hall
Kirkby Fleetham
Northallerton
North Yorkshire

Hambleton's Toasted Rice Pudding

1 pint milk
3 oz pudding rice
4 egg yolks
2 oz sugar
½ pint double cream
2 fl oz milk
vanilla and nutmeg

Cook the rice gently until tender.
Strain off any excess milk and put the rice aside.
Whisk the egg yolks and sugar then add all the other ingredients including the cooked rice.
Pour the mixture into a dish (the mixture should be about 1½ to 2 inches deep).
Place the dish into a bain marie. Cook for approximately 20 minutes at gas mark 4 or until the mixture has set, as per an egg custard.
Cut out shapes with a pastry cutter and 'toast' the top like a Creme Brulee.

Brian Baker
Hambleton Hall
Hambleton
Oakham
Rutland

Fresh Pineapple with Orange Syrup and Yoghurt

Though very simple, this makes an irresistible dessert, and even more so if you serve it with dark chocolate cake. In season you can add strawberries, raspberries, redcurrants or blackberries to this fruit salad. Just stir them in gently after mixing in the syrup.

Serves 6-8

1 large pineapple
juice of 3 small oranges
6 oz (175g) caster sugar
2 heaped tablespoons (3-4 x 15ml spoon) natural yoghurt

Slice the pineapple and cut off the skin; cut the flesh into largish pieces and put in a serving bowl. Put the orange juice in a saucepan, not too small, and add the caster sugar. Stir to dissolve the sugar over a low heat, then bring to the boil and boil fiercely for 3 minutes. Pour the hot syrup onto the pineapple pieces and stir thoroughly. Leave to cool. Shortly before serving stir in the yoghurt, just very roughly.

Josceline Dimbleby, food writer and author of several cookery books, including 'The Josceline Dimbleby Collection' a Sainsbury cookbook.

Amaretto flavoured Creme Brulee

Serves 6

1 measure Amaretto - almond liqueur
4 egg yolks
1 pint double cream
2 oz caster sugar
vanilla essence
demerara sugar to glaze

Scald (bring to boil) the cream and vanilla essence.
Lightly cream egg yolks and sugar in a large bowl.
Pour cream onto egg and sugar whilst whisking.
Return to the stove in a clean thick-bottomed pan and stirring continually, cook the mixture until it coats the back of a wooden spoon.
Add amaretto, strain through a fine sieve and pour the mixture into six ramekin dishes and leave to set.
When cold sprinkle the top with demerara sugar and glaze under a hot grill until all the sugar has melted and is golden brown.
Return to fridge and chill for 1 - 2 hours. Serve straight from the fridge.

To eat
Crack the sugar with a gentle tap using a teaspoon and eat the topping with the the cream.

This is an ideal sweet for dinner parties as it requires minimum cooking time and takes no time at all to serve leaving the hosts with more time to entertain their guests. Also, the recipe can be made without the amaretto and is still very successful.

Robert Elsmore
Hunstrete House
Hunstrete
Chelwood
Near Bristol
Avon

Treacle and Walnut Tart

Pastry:- 2 oz butter
         1 egg yolk
         2 oz icing sugar
         5 oz plain flour

Filling:- 3 eggs
          ¼ pint syrup
          3 tablespoons milk
          6 oz walnuts
          6 oz demerara sugar

Pastry

Combine all ingredients to form a sweet pastry. Put in refrigerator for 1 hour. Grease an 8 inch by 1 inch baking tin and line with rolled out pastry. Fill with baking beans and bake blind until golden brown on Gas Mark 4, 180 deg C, 350 deg F.

Filling

Bring the syrup and sugar to the boil and simmer for 2 minutes. Combine with eggs, milk and walnuts and mix together with the syrup and sugar. Fill the pastry case and bake in a low oven gas 2, 150 deg C, 300 deg F until the tart is firm.

Serve warm with fresh cream or vanilla sauce.

Nick Reed
Blostin's Restaurant
29 Waterloo Road
Shepton Mallet
Somerset

Bread and Butter Pudding

Makes 3 large souffle dishes

3 french bread sticks
soaked sultanas
9 eggs
6 yolks
1 tsp vanilla
12 oz caster sugar
27 fl oz milk
27 fl oz cream

Thinly slice the french sticks and butter.
Layer the bread in greased souffle dishes.
Sprinkle the soaked sultanas between layers.
Mix the eggs, yolks, vanilla and caster sugar.
Heat the milk and cream.
Add this to the egg mixture.
Strain and pour mixture onto puddings.
Bake for 45 minutes in a bain-marie at 325 deg. F.

Colin John Bussey
The Gleneagles Hotel
Auchterarder
Perthshire

Meringues with Passion Fruit and Oranges

2 egg whites
4 oz caster sugar

Beat egg whites until stiff, slowly beat in 2 oz caster sugar and then fold in remainder. Spoon out onto grease proofed trays and bake in low oven for one hour. Mark 1.

6 passion fruit
4 large oranges, segmented
2 oz honey

Bowl of whipped cream

Boil honey with a little water and a squeeze of lemon juice until a syrup. Add passion fruit and orange segments. Place two meringues on a plate and pipe a squirl of whipped cream. Pour sauce around and serve immediately.

Nicholas and Nicola Hayward
Seaview Hotel & Restaurant
The High Street
Seaview
Isle of Wight

Sticky Toffee Pudding

1 oz butter
3 oz caster sugar
3 oz chopped dates
3 oz self raising flour
1 level teaspoon bicarbonate soda
¾ pint water
1 egg
vanilla essence

Cream butter and sugar until light and fluffy. Add egg and then flour and then bicarbonate soda. Cook dates in water and then add to mixture. Add vanilla essence and mix well. Pour mixture in well greased baking tin (6ins x 8ins). Bake gas mark 4 for approximately 30 minutes.

Sauce:
Bring to the boil 2 pints of double cream and add 4 tablespoons of brown sugar and 1 tablespoon of black treacle. Allow to simmer for 5 minutes or until the sauce thickens slightly.

Francis Coulson and Brian Sack
Sharrow Bay Hotel
Lake Ullswater
Penrith
Cumbria

Creme Brulee

Serves 6

600 ml Double cream
1 pod vanilla
3 egg yolks
100g caster sugar
100g demerara sugar

Put three-quarters of the double cream in a heavy saucepan with the vanilla pod and bring to the boil. Mix the remaining cream well with the egg yolks and caster sugar and pour into the boiling cream. Stir constantly over a gentle heat until the mixture thickens, but do not allow it boil or it will curdle. Remove from the heat and allow to cool.
Discard the vanilla pod, then pour into individual heatproof dishes and chill in the refrigerator until set. Sprinkle a layer of demerara sugar over top of each dish and flash under a really hot grill so that the sugar caramelizes quickly. Chill again in the refrigerator before serving.

Richard Shepherd
Langans Brasserie
Stratton Street
Piccadilly
London

Arlequin Au Chocolat

1200 g melted warm white chocolate
800 g melted warm dark chocolate
1600 g creme patissier (room temperature)
4 litres single cream (ensure not too cold)
12 thin slices genoise sponge (cut 1" smaller than ring)
½ pint rum and stock syrup

Line six 8" flan rings with genoise. Dab with the rum and stock syrup mixture.
Take two large round bottomed bowls and divide the creme patissier between the two.
Divide the cream into two equal amounts and semi-whip.
Add the melted warm chocolate (dark) to one of the creme patissiers, whisking continually.
Then add half the cream (2 litres) to this mixture, whisking fast to start with and slowly towards the end, taking care not to overwhip.
Pour this mixture half way in the ring. Smooth out with a palette knife, place remaining genoise sponge on top, dab again with stock syrup and rum.
Follow the same method with the white chocolate. Smooth the top and place in the fridge.

Keith Stanley
The Ritz
Piccadilly
London

148

Chocolate Rum Truffle Cake

Sponge

3 eggs
2¾ oz caster sugar
2¾ oz flour
½ oz cocoa

Whisk eggs and sugar till thick and fluffy. Put half the mixture into
another bowl. Fold in 1½ oz sifted flour into one bowl and 1¼ oz flour and
½ oz cocoa into the other bowl. Line 12" x 9" swiss roll tin with non
stick parchment paper. Pipe diagonal alternate stripes of chocolate and
plain sponge. Bake at reg. 4 for 15 minutes. Turn out onto rack and cool.
Peel off paper. Or make a plain sponge.

Line 1½ pint oblong mould with cling film, cut sponge and line bottom and
sides of mould keeping one slice to top off with. Mix 2 tablsp. rum with 2
tablsp. of stock syrup and brush over sponge. Set aside.

Filling.

7 oz good quality chocolate, in small pieces
½ pint single cream
1 egg
1 tablsp rum

Put chocolate in blender goblet. Bring cream to boil. Add to chocolate
blend till smooth. Add egg and the rum. blend again. Set aside to cool.
When almost set pour into mould on top of sponge. Top off with last piece
of sponge. Fold over cling film. Chill overnight. Turn out and slice.

Joyce Molyneux
The Carved Angel
2 South Embankment
Dartmouth
Devon

Mousse Brulee

Vanilla essence
10 eggs separated
1 pint double cream
4 leaves gelatine
3 tablespoons caster sugar
8 oz granulated sugar
10 tablespoons water

Make a caramel by slowly bringing to the boil 8 oz granulated sugar and 5
tablespoons water, reserving a further five to finish caramel. In a mixer,
with whisk attachment, beat together egg yolks and caster sugar with a
little vanilla essence until white and creamy.
In a separate bowl beat double cream until thick but not stiff.

Soak gelatine in some cold water and set aside until caramel has started to go brown. When this happens, wait until a light brown colour appears and remove caramel from heat, carefully add further five tablespoons of water and allow caramel to cool for five minutes. Add gelatine to this and swill around pan until gelatine is dissolved.

With motor still running on mixer, pour the caramel into egg mixture, remove bowl from mixer and carefully add double cream into this.

Beat egg white until very thick but not too stiff and fold these carefully into mixture. Pour into souffle dishes to set for approximately five hours.

Dust each one with icing sugar and scorch with a hot poker minutes before serving.

Rogano Seafood Bar and Restaurant
11 Exchange Place
Glasgow

Biscuit Glace

2 eggs
100g Sugar
50g clear honey
70g glace cherries (finely chopped)
70g mixed peel (finely chopped)
175 ml whipping cream
80g praline

Cook sugar in a little water until it reaches (filet) stage (will create ribbon effect). Gently add honey. Whisk yolks and slowly add ½ of the sugar mixture. Whisk whites until stiff and add the other half of the sugar mixture. Fold both of these mixtures together, then fold in the cherries, mixed peel and praline.** Pour into ramekins and put in freezer. Allow at least 1 hour in the freezer and then serve.

** 1. Roast 80g of mixed nuts until golden brown
   2. Cook 100g of sugar in water until caramelised
   3. Mix 1 and 2 together
   4. When cold chop in the blender.

Oliver Godfrey
Le Grandgousier
15 Western Street
Brighton
Sussex

Creme Brulee or Burnt Cream

2 oz sugar
3 egg yolks
½ pint double cream
vanilla pod
Creme de Banane

Mix the sugar and egg yolks together and beat until light in colour and sugar has dissolved.

Add the cream, split the vanilla pod down the centre, remove the seeds with a knife and place the pod with the custard mixture.

At this stage you can flavour the brulee with any combination of the following: Creme de Banane
                Grand Marnier with orange
                Rum
                Passion Fruit
                Vanilla

Once you have added the flavouring, pour the custard mixture into small ramekin or earthenware pots and place these in a water bath or 'bain marie'. Place in the oven on 150 deg C, 300 deg F or gas mark 2 for approximately 30 minutes.

To test if cooked, you should touch the top of the brulees and see if they are set and that the custard is not runny. However do not overcook or the mixture will split.

Ron Maxfield
Cliveden
Taplow
Berkshire

Black Forest Gateau

Chocolate Genoise Sponge

5 whole eggs
1 egg yolk
5 oz sugar
4 oz flour
1 oz cocoa powder
1 oz melted butter

To decorate gateaux:
1 tin black cherries (no stones)
2 pints cream (whipped)
raspberry jam
chocolate vermicelli
plus bakers chocolate

Whip eggs, yolk and sugar to a thick foam, thick enough to run off whisk in a thick ribbon. Melt butter and sieve flour and cocoa meanwhile. Remove eggs from machine, lightly fold in flour and cocoa, last of all mix in butter. Treat very lightly and do not over mix. Put in 10" cake tin, bake at 425 degrees Fahrenheit till springy to touch or when it shrinks from side of tin. Leave to cool and set for a day before cutting. Cut into three, spread base with raspberry jam, then a thin layer of whipped cream. Slightly thicken the juice from a small tin of cherries, enough to set when cold, then when cold, add the cherries to it and put half onto cream on base of gateaux. Another thin layer of cream then next sponge. Sprinkle with Kirsch then repeat the process with cream and cherries. Put on top layer of sponge, cover with cream and chocolate decorations.

Karl Wadsack
The Three Lions
Stuckton
Fordingbridge
Hampshire

Sultana and Cinnamon Sponge

Serves 28

1 lb butter
1 lb sugar
8 eggs
1 lb 8 oz flour
2-3 oz cinnamon
6 oz sultanas
1 oz baking powder
2 pinches salt
14 fl oz milk

Cream butter and sugar until very white.
Add eggs, one at a time, beating well after adding each one.
Fold in flour, cinnamon, salt and baking powder.
Mix in milk.
Fold in sultanas.
Cook in steamer for approximately 15-20 minutes in buttered and papered ramekins.

Roast Pears

Cut poached pears into 8 even slices.
Sprinkle each slice with brown sugar and caramelize with a burner.

Pear Sauce

Using pear trimmings, liquidize with a little Poire William and stock syrup.
Pass through a fine sieve.
Correct consistency if necessary.
Serve warm around pudding.

Ramon Farthing
Calcot Manor
Near Tetbury
Gloucestershire

Carrot Cake with a Cream Cheese Filling

Makes one cake 6 - 8 portions

```
8 egg whites )
170g sugar   ) whisk to a full peak

8 egg yolks  )
170g sugar   ) whisk until stiff
```

400g ground hazelnuts
300g grated carrots

Grated zest of 2 lemons
50g flour

Mix together the whisked egg mixtures.
Gently add the carrots and hazelnuts.
Fold in the sieved flour and lemon zest.
Place in a lined greased baking tin and cook for one hour at 375 deg F.

When cooked allow to cool on a wire rack.

Cream Cheese Icing

To make the icing mix 250g cream cheese (philadelphia) with 150g of icing sugar and beat with a wooden spoon until soft.

To assemble the Cake

Slice the cake horizontally - into 3 and place the cream cheese between the layers like a sandwich, dust the top with icing sugar and decorate with marzipan carrots.

Graham Newbould
Inverlochy Castle
Torlundy
Fort William
Scotland

Mississippi Mud Cake

Very Rich

2 cups caster sugar
6 oz chocolate
8 oz butter
cup hot water
1/3rd cup whisky
1 tblsp coffee

2 eggs
1½ cup plain flour
½ cup self raising flour
2 tblsp cocoa

Melt first half of ingredients in double boiler. Cool slightly then add
remaining ingredients. Bake in moderate oven for roughly 1¼ hours (test,
springy on top to touch). Serve either hot with cream as dessert or cut
into squares as for a petit four.

James and Amanda Graham
Ostlers Close Restaurant
25 Bonnygate
Cupar
Fife

Strawberry Shortcake

8 oz plain flour
5 oz butter
2½ oz icing sugar
2 egg yolks
4-6 drops vanilla essence

1 lb strawberries (hulled)
½ pint double cream
caster sugar to taste
icing sugar

First sift the flour on to your working surface, make a well in the centre
and put in the butter, icing sugar, egg yolks, and 2-3 drops of vanilla
essence. Work these ingredients to a smooth paste, then set the mixture in
a cool place for 1 hour before using.
Set oven at 350 deg F or Mark 4. Divide the pastry in two, roll or pat out
into two 9 inch rounds, ¼ inch thick, place on a baking sheet and bake in
the preset oven for 15 - 20 minutes. Trim shortcake while still warm and
cut one round into eight sections. Cool on a wire rack.
Slice the strawberries, reserving eight whole ones for decoration. Whip
the cream, sweeten to taste, and add 2-3 drops of vanilla essence; put one-
third of the cream aside for decoration. Mix the sliced strawberries into
the remainder of the cream. Put the cream and fruit on the plain round of
shortcake, smooth over and arrange the sections of shortcake on the top.
Dust with icing sugar and decorate with rosettes of cream and reserved
strawberries.

Robin and Sheena Buchanan-Smith
Isle of Eriska
Ledaig
Oban
Argyll

155

Chocolate Marquis with Coffee Bean Sauce

Serves 10-16

For Marquis:
8 egg yolks   )
8 oz caster sugar) beaten together
5 oz plain chocolate - melted
5 oz cocoa powder)
10 oz butter   ) creamed
1 pint double cream - slightly beaten
20-30 Boudoir Biscuits
1 tablesp cognac   )
1 tablesp instant coffee) for Boudoir Dip
4 tablesp water   )

Coffee Bean Sauce:
6 egg yolks
3 oz caster sugar
1 pint milk
vanilla pod
1 heaped teaspoon ground coffee

Mix together all the ingredients of the Marquis in the following order:
Yolk and sugar well beaten, add to
The melted and cooled plain chocolate, and then
Beat the previous ingredients with the creamed cocoa powder and butter.
Finally, fold in the cream vigourously so that it is totally incorporated.
Dip the Boudoir Biscuits in the coffee/cognac mix and line a 3 pint souffle
dish. Gently place the total ingredients into the lined souffle mould.
Refrigerate for 3 hours. Dip in hot water and turn out on to a flat plate.
Cut with sharp knife dipped into hot water.

Coffee Bean Sauce:

Beat egg yolks with half the sugar until light and fluffy. Boil the milk,
coffee, vanilla pod and remaining sugar. After boiling point has been
reached remove from heat and allow to cool (about 10 minutes). Beat this
into the eggs/sugar mixture. Place the entire mixture back into the pan in
which you boiled the milk and place over a low heat. Continually stir,
WITHOUT LEAVING for about 8-12 minutes, or until the custard covers the
back of a silverspoon. Pour mixture into a porclain bowl and cover with
greaseproof paper. Cool.

Serving:
Slice Marquis as described and serve with a jug of the chilled custard.

Adrian Clarke
The Fox and Goose
Fressingfield
Diss
Norfolk

MISCELLANY

Arisaig House Breakfast Marmalade

Makes approximately 10lbs.

3 lb seville oranges
3 lemons
3 sweet oranges
6 pints water

Boil in preserving pot until the fruit is soft – at least half an hour.
Remove the fruit, cut in half. Remove the pulp and pips and return them to
the water. Reduce this liquor by half at a moderate simmer.
Chop the peel as small or finely as you would like it. I serve mine in
strips of about 1/8th inch by 1 inch.
Sieve the pulp and pips from the reduced liquor and discard them. Add
chopped peel and 6 lb preserving sugar or granulated sugar to the liquor
and boil till set. This may be tested more quickly by putting a little on
a cold dish in a refrigerator. Be careful not to boil too vigorously and
bring up to temperature slowly, while stirring, to ensure that the sugar
does not burn.
Ensure that your jam jars have been thoroughly cleaned and are hot when the
marmalade is poured into them. Cover while hot.

David Wilkinson
Arisaig House
Beasdale
Arisaig
Inverness-shire

Rochers (Swiss Meringue Petits Fours)

4 egg whites
250g caster sugar
150g browned almond flakes
juice of a lemon

Using a bain marie e.g. a Pyrex bowl over a pan of gently simmering water,
whisk the egg whites and caster sugar. The bowl should not actually be
touching the water as this will cause the whites to cook too quickly and
unevenly. This task is easier to perform with an electric hand whisk and
may take as long as 10 minutes, according to temperature. When the egg
whites and sugar are totally thick and firm (there must be no trace of
runniness) fold in the browned almonds when they have cooled and the lemon
juice. The mixture should be of a firm dropping consistency and should
hold its shape completely. Using two spoons apportion the mixture onto
silican baking parchment and cook in a cool oven at 150 deg f overnight for
at least 9 hours.

David Wilkinson
Arisaig House
Beasdale
Arisaig
Inverness-shire

Ginger Creams

680g ginger preserve
4 fl oz brandy
4 fl oz advocat
50 fl oz double whipping cream

Put ginger, brandy and advocat in bowl and whisk until creamy.
Gently whisk in cream then blend until stiff.
Put into small ramekins.

Oliver Godfrey
Le Grandgousier
15 Western Street
Brighton
Sussex

Mint Creams

1000g icing sugar
2 egg whites

peppermint essence
1 gill double cream

Put egg whites, essence and cream into blender - gently blend adding sugar
slowly - blend until stiff.

Pipe onto greaseproof paper. Leave until surface of mint is dry, then cut
into pieces.

Oliver Godfrey
Le Grandgousier
15 Western Street
Brighton
Sussex

Rum Truffles

1 lb dark chocolate
2 egg yolks
½ pint double cream
3 fl oz dark rum
cocoa powder

Break up the chocolate and melt in a double boiler. Add the egg yolks,
cream and rum, beat for three or four minutes. Allow to set in the fridge.
Using a spoon scoop out and roll into a ball and then dip in the cocoa
powder.

Stephen Smith
The Belvedere Hotel
19 North Park Road
Bradford
West Yorkshire

Peanut Flower Cookies

Makes about 80 cookies

5 oz (140g) butter
8 oz (225g) caster sugar
1 large egg, beaten
5 oz (140g) smooth peanut butter
½ tsp vanilla
7 oz (200g) plain flour
1 tsp baking powder
½ tsp salt

Cream the butter and sugar together until smooth, light and soft.
Beat in first the egg, then the peanut butter and vanilla.
Sift the flour with the baking powder and salt and stir into the mixture.
Roll all but one large tablespoon of the mixture into marble-sized balls
with the fingers and put, well apart, on three ungreased baking sheets.
With a sharp small knife cut each ball across, as if to cut it in half, but
without cutting more than halfway through the ball. Repeat the cut at
right angles so that the ball now has four segments.
Gently ease the four 'petals' open. Make a tiny ball from the reserved
mixture and put into the middle of the 'flower', like a bud.
Bake for 12 minutes or until pale brown.
While hot, gently ease off the baking sheet and lift, with a palette knife
or fish slice, on to a cooling rack.
Store in an airtight container.

Pru Leith, owner of Leith's Restaurant and Leith's School of Food and Wine,
both in London. She has also written many cookery books and articles in
magazines such as Taste.

Salade Aphrodite

A fine salad of aphrodisiacs from around the world.

Serves 4

2 whole lobsters (cooked and cleaned)
360mls fish jelly
80g fresh crab (cooked and cleaned)
4 oysters
50g celeriac - fine strips
50g mushrooms - fine batons
80g truffle - fine strips
corn salad
2 artichokes
4 quail eggs
16 asparagus heads
4 teaspoons lobster mayonnaise
40g caviar
20g salmon eggs
chives

Melt fish jelly until dissolved.
Pour small amount onto plate.
Place the caviar and salmon eggs onto the plate and mix in a figure of
eight until evenly dispersed throughout.
Leave to set.
Take artichoke, cut in half and slice thinly.
Open oysters.
Using the escalopes of artichoke make a circle to be used as the base of
the salad.
Place the oyster in the middle of the circle.
Then place some salad on top of base of artichoke.
Using the white part of the mushroom (the cap) make thin batons.
Squeeze a little lemon juice on them so as not to discolour.
Finely slice the celeriac and make into strips.
Mix this into the mushroom.
Slice the cooked asparagus into quarters (lengthways) and add to the
mixture.
Cut lobster into thick slices.
Mix lobster and crab into the mixture and season to taste.
Assemble this mixture on top of the artichoke base as neatly as possible.
Slice the truffle as for the celeriac.
Place the quail egg at the top of the salad.
Taking extreme care garnish the salad with corn salad and chives.
Place a teaspoon of the lobster mayonnaise onto the egg.
Sprinkle the fine strips of truffle over the mayonnaise.
Readjust the garnish if required, taking extreme care.

Quail Eggs

Place whole egg in boiling water and cook for 1½ minutes. After this time
plunge into iced water. When cold peel and leave in cold water until
required.

Artichokes

Cut off the stalk and pull out all the underneath leaves.
With a large knife cut through the artichoke leaving only 1½ cm at the
bottom of the vegetable.
With a small sharp knife, whilst holding the artichoke upside down, peel
carefully, removing all the leaf and any green part, keeping the bottom as
smooth as possible.
Rub with a lemon and keep in a lemon water solution.
Artichokes should always be cooked in a blanc.
Once cooked remove choke.

Blanc

½ litre cold water
10g flour
½ lemon (juice only)
salt

Mix the flour and water together.
Add the salt and lemon juice.
Place in a pan, bring to the boil, stirring continuously.

Chicken stock

250g chicken carcasses
OR
½ boiling fowl

25g carrots
¼ leek (white base only)
¼ celery
25g mushrooms
½ onion
1 clove
1 bouquet garni
5g butter

Sweat the finely sliced vegetables in a pan with the butter. Add the
carcasses or boiling fowl. Cover with the cold water and bring to the
boil. Lower the heat and simmer gently, skimming the surface frequently.
After 10 minutes cooking time add the onion, spiked with the clove, and
bouquet garni. Cook for a further 2 hours, then strain the stock into a
bowl through a muslin lined sieve. Leave to cool.

Fish Stock

250g fish bones (e.g sole, turbot, whiting or any white fleshed fish)
10g onion
¼ leek (use white base only)
10g mushrooms
10g butter
25ml dry white wine

1 bouquet garni
½ litre water

Soak the bones in cold water for 2 hours.
Roughly chop the fish bones. Wash and chop the vegetables and sweat them
in the butter. Add the chopped bones and simmer for a few minutes. Pour
in the white wine, increase the heat and reduce the liquid by half, then
cover the contents of the pan with water. Bring to the boil skimming the
surface frequently.
After 5 minutes cooking time, add the bouquet garni and simmer uncovered
for 20 minutes. Carefully strain the stock into a bowl through a muslin-
lined sieve. Leave to cool.

Gelee- fish stock

500ml chicken stock
500ml fish stock
6 egg whites
100g meat (minced)
100g fish (minced)
1 bayleaf
15 leaves gelatine
5g chicken bouillon powder
salt and pepper to taste

Place minced meat and fish into a large pan. Combine with egg whites,
bouillon powder, salt and pepper and bayleaf. Add the cold fish and
chicken stock to mixture. Place over a high heat stirring frequently to
avoid burning. The impurities will rise to the surface and a crust will
then begin to form.

Whilst this is taking place soak the gelatine in water for 15 minutes.
Make a small hole towards the centre of the crust, thus enabling impurities
to rise more freely to the surface. Skim frequently and simmer gently for
a further 15 - 20 minutes. When the stock has cleared add the soaked
gelatine and cook for a further 5 minutes.
Strain through a muslin lined sieve taking extreme care not to disturb the
crust on the gelee. Leave to cool.

Lobster Sauce - for mayonnaise

250g lobster   20g flour
20g butter or oil   25g tomato puree
25g celery   350ml fish stock
25g onion   30ml dry white wine
25g carrot   1 bouquet garni
15ml brandy   ½ crushed clove garlic
salt

Well wash the lobster.
Cut in half lengthwise, head first, then the tail.
Discard the sac from the head, clean the entrails from the tail.
Wash the lobster pieces.

Crack the claws and the four claw joints.
Melt butter in a pan.
Add the lobster pieces and the vegetables.
Allow to cook without colouring.
Add the brandy and allow it to ignite.
Remove from the heat, mix in the flour and tomato puree.
Return to a gently heat and cook out flour.
Cool slightly, gradually add the fish stock and white wine.
Stir to the boil.
Add bouquet garni, garlic and season lightly with salt.
Simmer for 15 - 20 minutes.
Remove the lobster pieces.
Remove the lobster meat from the pieces.
Crush the lobster shells, return to the pan and cook for ¼ - ¾ hour.
Pass through a course strainer.

Mayonnaise

2 egg yolks
2 teaspoons white wine vinegar
salt to taste
ground white pepper to taste
1/8th teaspoon English mustard
250ml olive oil
1 teaspoon boiling water

Place yolks, vinegar, mustard, seasoning in a bowl and whisk well.
Gradually pour oil, very slowly, whisking continuously.
Add the boiling water, whisking well. Correct seasoning.

Lobster mayonnaise

Combine mayonnaise with lobster sauce at the ratio of 2 parts sauce to 1
part mayonnaise.

Kevin Cape
The Bell Inn
Aston Clinton
Buckinghamshire

164

Cheese Straws

2 oz plain flour (50g)
2 oz grated Parmesan cheese (50g)
2 oz butter (room temperature) (50g)
¼ teasp salt
1 pinch cayenne pepper
1 twist ground black pepper
2 oz grated Cheshire cheese (50g)
For topping:- garlic salt, celery salt, mild curry powder, cayenne

Pre-heat oven to gas mark 5 (375F) (190C)
Grease a baking sheet. Then sift the flour into a bowl and add the salt, cayenne and black pepper. Next add the Parmesan cheese and butter and rub the mixture to the crumbly stage. Now, using a fork, stir in the grated Cheshire cheese then, using your hands, bring the mixture together to form a dough. As Cheshire cheese is usually fairly moist you should not need any liquid, but, if it seems dry, add just a spot of milk. Then roll the dough out fairly thinly to a thickness of around 1/8th inch (3mm) and, using a small 1 or 1½ inch (2.5 or 4cm) cutter, cut the biscuits out and arrange them on the greased baking sheet. They do not spread during the cooking so you can arrange them fairly close together. Leave them plain if you like or sprinkle them with any of the suggested toppings above. Bake the biscuits for 10-12 minutes on a high shelf then remove them to a cooling rack to cool and crisp.

Robin and Sheena Buchanan-Smith
Isle of Eriska
Ledaig
Oban
Argyll

Dauphinoise Potatoes

Approximately 1 lb potatoes (peeled, sliced very thinly but no washed)
6 fl oz heavy cream
6 oz grated Gruyere or Emmenthal
1 clove garlic
salt, fresh milled black pepper.

Put a little cream in the bottom of a shallow ceramic dish with a clove of garlic, place a layer of potato slices just overlapping, on this sprinkle some cheese add a little cream and season, repeat the process until you have four layers of potato with cheese on top and the last of the cream. Bake in a hot oven 420 deg C until cooked and brown and bubbling. Check with the point of a knife, should take approximately 15 -20 minutes.

Stephen and Anne Frost
The Stonor Arms
Stonor
Nr Henley-on-Thames
Oxfordshire

Carrots with Ginger, Lemon and Honey

Adding a pinch of sugar and a dash of lemon to the cooking water of carrots is a well-known enhancer. This recipe goes several steps further, replacing sugar with honey, scenting the carrots with a waft of ginger. It's good enough to eat on its own, but goes well with plainly grilled chicken, too.

Serves 6-8

1 lemon
1 tblsp, honey
1" piece of ginger, peeled and sliced
2 oz butter
2 lbs carrots, sliced thinly
salt

Pare the zest of the lemon in thin strips with a potato peeler. Squeeze the juice. Put the zest and juice into the blender with the honey, ginger, and ¼ pint of water. Liquidise and strain.
Melt the butter in a large frying pan, and saute the carrots lightly. Add the contents of the blender, and salt, bring up to the boil, cover and cook gently until just tender. The carrots should absorb nearly all the liquid, but if necessary, uncover and boil hard to reduce to a buttery glaze.

Joyce Molyneux
The Carved Angel
2 South Embankment
Dartmouth
South Devon

Mango Chutney

Makes approximately 1½ lbs.

1 lb mangoes   6 oz onions
8 oz cooking apples   1 pint spiced vinegar
½ teaspoon salt   1 teaspoon ground ginger
10 oz brown sugar

Slice the mangoes. Peel, core and slice the apples and put in a bowl with the mangoes. Sprinkle with salt and leave overnight. Next day rinse and drain. Peel and finely chop the onions and put in a saucepan with the mangoes and apples, vinegar and ginger. Bring to the boil and simmer gently until the fruit and onions are soft. Add the sugar and stir until it has dissolved. Continue simmering, stirring occasionally until the chutney is very thick. Pot into warm jars and seal.

Stephen Smith
Belvedere Hotel
19 North Park Road
Bradford
West Yorkshire

166

Basic Stock Syrup

2lb (900g) preserving or cube sugar
1 pint (600ml) water

Simply dissolve the sugar in the water over a low heat in a very clean saucepan and infuse at first over this same low heat. Then turn up the heat and allow the liquid to simmer for about 15 minutes.

John Tovey

Bechamel Sauce

Makes about 15 fl oz (450ml)

1½ oz (40g) butter
1½ oz (40g) white or wholemeal flour
15 fl oz (450ml) skimmed or semi-skimmed milk
1 blade mace (optional)
1 bay leaf
1 shallot, very finely chopped
pinch of salt, freshly ground black pepper

Melt the butter in a heavy saucepan, stir in the flour and cook for 2 minutes on a very low heat. This stage is very important because if the flour is not thoroughly cooked, the sauce will have a strong floury flavour.
Slide the pan off the heat and whisk in a little milk with a balloon whisk. Add the rest of the milk a little at a time, whisking constantly so that there are no lumps. Now return the sauce to the heat, add the mace (if using), bay leaf and finely chopped shallot, bring up to just under simmering point and cook for 10 minutes, stirring all the time. Season to taste and remove the bay leaf.

Susan Hicks

5 Herb Sauce

Equal quantities (approximately 4 oz) of

Sorrel   Tarragon
Basil   Chervil
Flat Parsley

1 litre Olive Oil

Finely chop the herbs then add to the olive oil. Leave for 1 hour at room temperature. It is then ready for use. Ideal for fish.

Oliver Godfrey
Le Grandgousier
15 Western Street
Brighton

Chilli Sauce

Using a bechamel sauce as a base, add a dessertspoon of tomato puree and tabasco to taste.

Then add: 2 chillis (chopped fresh or ready chopped) or one teasp chilli
powder
Splash Worcester sauce and splash red wine
Teaspoon English mustard
4 gherkins (sliced small)
3 freshly chopped tomatoes

Simmer on a very low heat for approximately 15 minutes to bring out the flavours. If the Sauce appears to lose too much moisture replace with a little cream, red wine or water.

Steven P Saunders
The Pink Geranium
Melbourn
Royston
Hertfordshire

Bread Sauce

1 onion studded with 2 cloves
2 oz breadcrumbs
1 bay leaf
1 oz butter
½ pint milk
seasoning
pinch mace and nutmeg

Put the onion, mace, nutmeg, bay leaf and milk in a pan.
Simmer gently for 30 minutes. Strain and sprinkle the breadcrumbs onto the milk.

Leave to infuse for 15 minutes. Heat the sauce through, beat in a little butter, season and serve hot.

Ron Maxfield
Cliveden
Taplow
Berkshire

168

Sorrel and Basil Sauce

1 small onion chopped
5 fl oz (150ml) well flavoured fish stock
¾ fl oz (20ml) white wine vinegar
5 sweet basil leaves
10 sorrel leaves
2 spinach leaves
½ tsp. soy sauce
1 oz unsalted butter
1 fl oz (30ml) double cream
1.5 fl oz (45ml) yoghurt

Place the chopped onion, stock and white wine vinegar in a small pan.
Bring to the boil and reduce by about three quarters. Put all the other
ingredients in a liquidiser and add the reduction complete with onions.
Liquidise at top speed until smooth and turn out and keep cool until
required.

Can be served with fish - preferably salmon.

Oliver Godfrey
Le Grandgousier
15 Western Street
Brighton

Cucumber Sauce

1 large cucumber
2 oz butter
1 level teaspoon plain flour
1 tablespoon white wine vinegar
¼ pint fish stock
2 teaspoons finely chopped fresh tarragon
salt and pepper

Thinly peel the skin from the cucumber using potato peeler. Cut the
cucumber in half lengthways; scoop out the seeds with a teaspoon and
discard them. Finely chop the cucumber. Melt butter in pan, stir in the
sliced cucumber until soft. Blend in the flour with the vinegar and stir
in the fish stock - then stir this into the cucumber and add the tarragon.
Season and bring to the boil.

Makes approximately ½ pint.

Oliver Godfrey
Le Grandgousier
15 Western Street
Brighton

Sauce Jacqueline

Serves 4

250g carrots
150ml fish stock
½ clove garlic
salt
cayenne pepper
150ml cream
50ml sweet white wine (Sauternes)
lemon juice to taste
40g butter
40g brunoise of vegetables

Dice the carrot, place in a pan with stock, garlic and seasoning.
Simmer until carrots are cooked through, add the cream.
Cook out slowly, add Sauternes and simmer for 5 mins.
Liquidise and pass through a chinois.
The liquid should be retained as the sauce and the pulp discarded.
Blanch the brunoise and add to the sauce, monte with butter.
Season and add lemon juice to taste.

Colin John Bussey
The Gleneagles Hotel
Auchterarder
Perthshire

Marmalade D'Oignons

2 lb onions, finely sliced
4 tablespoons olive oil
4 oz caster sugar
10fl oz (300ml) white wine vinegar
4 cloves, 2 bayleaves
1 teaspoon ground black pepper
1 teaspoon salt
2 tablespoons tomato puree
large pinch cayenne

Saute onions in oil until translucent, add all other ingredients, cover and
cook gently for one hour. Check all seasonings, sugar, salt, pepper.
Continue cooking until a marmalade consistency has been reached. Cool.
Pour off oil, store in jars in a fridge.

Kevin Cape
The Bell Inn
Aston Clinton
Buckinghamshire

Herb Oil

Take a bunch of fresh herbs of your choice, put them in a clean jam jar and then fill up the jar with a light oil such as safflower (olive oil already has a strong distinctive flavour). Cover the jar and leave it in a warm place for about 3 weeks. Then remove the herbs (which will have become blackish) and strain carefully through kitchen or coffee filter paper. The oil will now have a lovely green colour and can be stored in a bottle in a cool dark place for several months. Use to enhance all kinds of barbecued fish or meat, or salads.

Alternative Mayonnaise

For those who are concerned about the risk factor in using raw egg yolks in conventional mayonnaise, it is now possible to buy pasteurised eggs from leading supermarkets and food halls. Alternatively, here is Mrs Beeton's recipe for a 'cooked' mayonnaise.

1 tablespoon salad oil
1 tablespoon sugar
1 teaspoon salt
1 dessertspoon mustard
3 egg yolks, lightly beaten
10 fl oz (300ml) milk or single cream
5 fl oz (150ml) white wine vinegar

Mix the oil, sugar, salt and mustard together in a basin. Add the lightly beaten egg yolks, then the milk or cream and then the vinegar. Put the mixture in a double boiler or in a basin set over a pan of simmering water and cook, stirring constantly, until a thick creamy consistency is achieved. Do not allow the mixture to boil. Cool and refrigerate until needed.

Susan Hicks. After her very successful BBC TV series and accompanying book, The Fish Course, Susan has now written The Main Course. She lives on The Isles of Scilly.

VICTORIAN BREAKFAST

Buck's Fizz

* * *

Fresh Chilled Grapefruit with Creme de Menthe

* * *

Porridge with Whisky, Demerara Sugar and Butter

* * *

Creamed Smoked Haddock in Puff Pastry

* * *

Devilled Kidneys
Glass of Claret

* * *

Hearty Lakeland Platter of Bacon, Egg, Sausage,
Tomato, Fried Bread, Apple, Mushroom, and Potato
Glass of Burgundy or Beaujolais

* * *

Toast and Baps with Home-made Strawberry Jam,
Marmalade and Honey

* * *

Coffee and Tea

John Tovey's Victorian Breakfast

Sunday is my day off during the season and I occasionally decide to invite guests round at 11.30 for 12.00 midday and serve a relatively easy 6-course meal.. It is popular as it allows everybody (including myself) to sleep in longer than usual, have a quick skim of the newspapers and then slowly socialize. Very civilized indeed.

To serve this meal successfully you want to do as much preparation as possible beforehand, and be really and truly organized for when the guests arrive.

Make sure you have the table attractively laid with cutlery, napkins etc, the day before and have one good sensibly-sized double saucepan ready for the prepared porridge and another for the smoked haddock.

You will need plates decorated with doyleys and some flowers for the grapefruit, liners for the porridge dishes, warmed plates for the smoked haddock, plates with doyleys only for the devilled kidneys (provided you intend to serve them in small dishes) and, of course, warmed plates for the Lakeland Platter. Don't forget to set your jam, marmalade and honey out in preserve dishes along with your butter portions and whatever you do, see the coffee machine is prepared and the teapot is to hand well before the arrival of the guests.

I greet my guests with a Buck's Fizz which I make up of half a glass of fresh orange juice topped up with sparkling white Burgundy (instead of the traditional Champagne), and this certainly gets them all smiling. I serve a small glass of inexpensive claret with the kidneys and then everybody thinks it daringly different to sup glasses of hearty Beaujolais with their fried platter! If it sounds revolting. I can assure you it isn't.

Fresh Chilled Grapefruit with Creme de Menthe

Per person

1 grapefruit
1 tablespoon Creme de Menthe
sprig of fresh mint

Criss-cross around the 'equator' of the grapefruit so that it falls into two attractively 'vandyked' halves. Remove the segments from each half and fill one half with all the flesh. Serve the half grapefruit on a plate decorated with a doyley and a fern, and some sprigs of fresh mint add colour. Just before serving, sprinkle generously with chilled Creme de Menthe.

Porridge with Whisky, Demerara Sugar and Butter

Per person

approximately 2 oz (50g) oats (but see my method)
generous ¼ pint (150ml) milk
a pinch of salt (optional)
½ tablespoon demerara sugar
½ tablespoon whisky
knob butter

Use any commercial oats – even the quick ones which 'cook in a minute'.
The amount the manufacturers recommend for 2 generous servings will serve 4
portions (don't forget this is a 6-course breakfast!). Use all milk
instead of water.

Whatever the quality of the oats, they are always the better for soaking
overnight in the milk. Cook the oats slowly in the milk (adding a little
salt if you like) for the length of the time stated on the packet, and when
cooked, keep warm in a double saucepan.

Serve the porridge in attractive soup cups or bowls. Sprinkle generously
with the demerara sugar, and a good helping of whisky (I use malt which, to
many people, is sacrilegious!), and finish off with a generous knob of
butter.

Creamed Smoked Haddock in Puff Pastry

Per person

a 3½ inch (9cm) vol au vent (see recipe below)
2 oz (50g) creamed haddock filling (see recipe below)

Make up a ½ batch of puff pastry (see recipe below) and roll it out to
1/8th inch (3mm) thickness. Cut into circles with a fluted cutter, chill
and then bake blind at 425 deg F (220 deg C) Gas 7. When ready to serve,
split each round in 2 (don't forget to throw away any soggy pastry) and
gently warm through again. Lightly pack the fillets of smoked haddock in
sufficient milk to cover them, and simmer slowly until the fish is cooked,
(See recipe for fuller instructions). Make a cheese sauce with the milk,
and at the last minute, combine the flaked fish with the sauce. After
warming through in a double saucepan (about twenty minutes) fill the pastry
with the smoked haddock and brush the lid with melted butter just before
serving. A wedge of fresh tomato either side of the pastry looks
attractive and a large sprig of fresh parsley completes the scene!

My Nan's Rough Puff Pastry

This is a rough puff pastry that does away with the endless resting in
between turns. It can be made up in about 10 minutes (a 1 lb (450g) mixing
produces 60 small mince pies at Christmas), and it can be done in a kitchen
at any temperature. The only process you will develop skill in is the use
of the rolling pin but I am quite confident that even on your first attempt
you will be on to a winner.
I normally prepare two separate 1 lb (450g) mixings as I find the short
rest one mixing has while I work on the other gives a slightly better edge
to the end result. So I suggest you double up the following basic recipe,
and use two separate bowls.

1 lb (450g) strong plain flour
generous pinch of salt
½ lb (225g) soft margarine
½ lb (225g) soft American lard, or shortening
1 tablespoon lemon juice made up to ½ pint (300ml) with very cold water

Having sieved the two lots of strong plain flour into the two bowls, you break up the fats into ½ oz (15g) pieces and dot them about over the flour. Shake the bowls separately in order to coat the pieces of fat with flour, and then gently make a well in the centre of each. Into this you pour the very cold water and lemon juice. Using a palette knife, mix together your basic doughs. They certainly don't look very attractive at this stage, and look uneven with pockets of flour and glaring areas of pure fat showing through. But don't worry.

Lightly flour a large rolling area and turn out the first dough mixing taking care to scrape out all the ingredients, however untidy this may look. Shape this basic dough gently into the shape of a house brick with the short end of the brick nearest you and long sides running down from your left to your right side.

Now you must take care. Hold the rolling pin at each end - never in the middle - and treat it with delicacy. If you attack the dough like a steam roller pounding over asphalt, the end result will be similar. Just tap the merest outline of the rolling pin in the middle, top and bottom of the 'brick' and then, starting at the impression immediately in front of you, just lightly - oh so lightly - give the rolling pin a good gentle push and remove your hands. (Imagine you are helping to start off a large snowball from the top of a hill).

Never bring the rolling pin back towards you with any pressure. Always make sharp, soft movements away from you, slowly but surely stretching the pastry out into a shape roughly measuring 16 x 5 inches (40 x 12 cm). Picture this long rectangle in three equal parts and fold the piece facing you up and over the middle third and bring the top down on top of these two thirds. You want this pastry to be as light as possible, so trap the air at this stage by gently tapping down on the three open layers at the short ends at your left and right. Give this piece of dough a quarter turn - imagine your dough is the hour hand pointing at 6 o'clock, and turn it to 9 o'clock. Put it to one side.

Now repeat the process with the second mixing of dough.

At the end of this first rolling the dough will have a slightly smoother consistency and will be easier to handle. Repeat this process three more times, flouring your work area well between each rolling so the dough does not stick. You may find when you turn the bottom third of dough up over the middle third there is a surplus of flour. I find a household 6-inch (15-cm) paintbrush useful here to brush the surplus flour away.

With each rolling, the texture becomes smoother and smoother. On the fourth and last rolling, the dough is even slightly resistant, so don't force it in any way. Sometimes it just will not roll to above measurements so, whatever you do, don't force it to this size at the expense of knocking the air out!

Pop the two doughs into separate polythene bags and leave to chill.

Rolling and Baking Rough Puff Pastry

When you take the rough puff pastry out of the freezer or fridge, make certain it comes back to a workable consistency before you start rolling it (out of a normal fridge, this should take 20 to 30 minutes, longer from a freezer).

You need a clean flat surface and a large rolling pin. Flour both of these well and roll the pastry out to about 1/8th inch (3mm) thickness. Cut out your shapes - squares or rounds - place them on slightly dampened metal trays, and put back in the fridge to chill. When you wish to cook them, remove from the fridge and put a piece of well-buttered greaseproof paper on top (greased side down on to the prepared pastry). Prick through the paper and pastry with a sharp pointed knife (about 6 pricks to a 3½ inch (9cm) vol au vent) and put immediately into a hot oven at 450 deg F (230 deg C) Gas 8. Unless I know the exact size of pastry you are cooking, it is impossible to tell you how long it will take to cook, but after about 12 minutes have a look and see how it is getting on. It is better to slightly overcook puff pastry and get it really brown and crisp, than undercook it.

The secret of success in serving puff pastry is how little you actually put on the serving plate and how much you throw away. When the pastry is absolutely cooked, split it in two and if there are any layers of slightly greasy pastry, gently tear them off and discard. You will then be left with ethereal puff pastry.

Vol Au Vents

I never make traditional vol au vents, but cut out fluted rounds and when cooked slice them across the middle. One circle is used as a base, the filling put on top of this at the very last minute (so many people combine the puff pastry and filling early on in the day, warm them through before serving, and wonder why the pastry has gone soggy!), and top off with the top of the pastry round. I then usually lightly paint the top with melted butter to add the finishing touch!

Finnan Haddock

Do be careful when buying finnan haddock. So much 'smoked' haddock these days is purely and simply dyed, and when you cook it in milk the fish gets paler and paler, and the milk more and more orange! Always try to buy it on the bone as I have nearly always found this to be the genuine article. On the bone allow 6 oz (175g) each for a fish course portion and 8 oz (225g) for a main course.

Smoked Haddock in Cheese Sauce

Serves 4 - 6

2 lb (1 kg) smoked finnan haddock
1½ pints (900 ml) milk
a few fresh parsley stalks
a couple of onion rings
8 peppercorns

Place the haddock in a baking dish that will take the fish in one layer and add enough milk to cover. Add the parsley, a couple of onion rings (no more), and the peppercorns.
Bake slowly in the oven at 300 deg F (150 deg C) Gas 2, for about 45 minutes. Remove the fish from the milk (retaining the milk) and flake the flesh off the bone into a bowl.
Pass the milk through a strainer and use it for making a Cheese Sauce (to each pint (600ml) of milk for the basic white sauce, add 4 oz (100g) finely

176

grated Cheddar cheese). Fold the haddock into the finished sauce and cover
with a butter wrapping (never throw away butter wrappings as they are ideal
for putting, inside down, on top of the sauces, and can be used for storing
pastry and cooked root vegetables)

To warm through, place the bowl of haddock and sauce into a bain marie with
boiling water, and place in a medium oven at 350 deg F (180 deg C), Gas 4,
for about 30 minutes. You can also warm it through in a double saucepan
which takes about 30 minutes. Then portion it out onto plates piped with
mashed potato to make a 'nest' for the fish, or just put into ramekins
which can be topped off with a little mashed potato and flashed under a hot
grill.

You can also use smoked haddock and cheese sauce with puff pastry rounds,
with pancakes or gougeres, or simply serve it by itself in ramekins with
soldier strips of hot buttered toast. If you feel extravagant, you can add
a couple of tablespoons of cooking brandy to the sauce, and I occasionally
fold in some sultanas that have been soaked overnight in brandy. But
always, always, fill your pastry at the last minute.

Devilled Kidneys

Per person

1 kidney
1 dessertspoon chopped onion
1 oz (25g) butter
½ teaspoon French mustard
1 tablespoon brandy

Prepare the kidneys carefully, making sure that the skin is removed and the
core is taken out.

Saute the finely chopped onion in the butter and add a little French
mustard. Pop in the kidneys, and seal well and then turn down the heat and
simmer slowly for about 3 or 4 minutes.

Flambe with cooking brandy (turn up the heat and add the brandy which
will catch fire and flame for a minute or so). Put the kidneys into
indiviual warmed dishes and sprinkle with chopped parsley.

Hearty Lakeland Platter

Per person

1 rasher bacon
1 sausage
1 slice apple
½ tomato
1 triangle fried bread
2 medium mushrooms
about ¼ potato, sliced (depending on size)
1 egg

For this you need 4 baking trays (or as many as you can fit into your
oven).

1. Lay rashers of your particular brand of smoked bacon on the tray (if you

prefer to leave the rind on make small snips all along the edge to stop the rasher from curling up).

2. Lay out (and prick) your favourite sausages.

3. Core and peel an apple and lay slices on a well-buttered tray.

4. Cut the tomatoes in half, brush with melted butter, and season with salt, sugar and freshly ground black pepper.

These are then ready for cooking in an oven set at 350 deg F (180 deg C), Gas 4, in the following order:-
Sausages   about 30 minutes
Bacon   about 15 minutes
Apple   about 10 minutes
Tomato   about 5 minutes

The fried bread can be done earlier. Cut however many portions you want, soak them in melted butter, and bake in the oven until slightly brown and crisp. Leave aside in the warming oven on kitchen paper.
  Mushrooms should be skinned and prepared and then at the last minute tossed off in butter.
  Potatoes should be partly boiled first and then fried off in butter at the last minute too.
  Eggs accordingly to taste (scrambled are often the easiest for 6 or more people).

John Tovey
Miller Howe Hotel
Windermere
English Lakes

AFTERNOON TEA

"The cup that cheers but not inebriates."

The tea plant is a small evergreen shrub of the Camellia family, from which
the young leaves are plucked and dried. We make our 'pot of tea' by
steeping the dried leaves in boiling water. The water must be fresh and
boiling fiercely, for if it has been re-heated or only simmering the
flavour will be stale and flat.

Most of the tea drunk in Britain is imported from India, China and Sri
Lanka (Ceylon). Below are some of the most popular teas available here:-

Assam
 From North East India it is typically a strong, rich liquor, full of body
and very economical.

Ceylon
  Quite light with an attractive character and smooth flavour, blends well
with Assam. Try a mixture of two parts Ceylon to one part Assam as a
start; if you want more colour and strength increase the proportion of
Assam.

Darjeeling
  A delicate Indian tea, delicious with milk or a slice of lemon. Tea from
this area is rightly called the champagne of teas.

Earl Grey
  A Keemun tea from China, scented with Oil of Bergamot. This pleasing and
established tea can be enjoyed with or without milk.

Keemun
  A mild tea with an attractive, delicate flavour. Suitable for drinking
with or without milk.

Lapsang Souchong
  From China, these teas have an easily recognisable tarry character. A
small pinch in a pot of Assam or Ceylon/Assam blend produces just a hint of
this renowned characteristic. A connoisseur's drink on its own.

Jasmine Tea
  Possibly the most refreshing tea on a hot day, this China tea is scented
with Jasmine flowers. It has a delicate flavour which is probably best
enjoyed without milk. As with Keemun and Darjeeling, this tea is becoming
increasingly popular in the evening or after meals.

John Goodwin Real Teas
High Street
Baldock
Hertfordshire

Farm Fruit Cake

6 oz (175g) wholewheat flour
6 oz (175g) plain flour
3 teaspoons baking powder
a pinch of salt
2 teaspoons ground nutmeg
5 oz (150g) butter
4 oz (100g) soft brown sugar
8 oz (225g) sultanas
4 oz (100g) mixed peel
2 oz (50g) glace cherries, chopped finely
juice and rind of 1 lemon
4 eggs
¼ pint (150ml) milk
blanched almonds for top of cake

Use a 10 inch (25cm) round cake tin and double-line it with greaseproof
paper. Pre-heat the oven to 350 deg F (180 deg C) gas 4.
Mix flours with the baking powder, salt and nutmeg and rub in the butter.
Fold in the sugar along with the sultanas, mixed peel and cherries. Add
the rind and juice of the lemon, then add the eggs that have been beaten
lightly with the milk.
This forms a paste which you put in the prepared cake tin and bake in the
pre-heated oven for 1½ hours.

Whipped Cream Cake

8 fl oz (225ml) double cream
3 eggs, lightly beaten
8 oz (225g) sieved self-raising flour
8 oz (225g) caster sugar
½ teaspoon salt
1 teaspoon vanilla essence

This is an extremely rich type of sponge cake, but made with whipped double
cream and no butter. It rises well and is filling. When soaked liberally
with liqueurs or spirits it is good served as a dessert, but I prefer it
for afternoon tea, filled with whipped cream and either jam or soft fruits.

In a large bowl, whip the double cream until fairly stiff and then fold in
the gently beaten eggs. Using a large metal spoon, gently fold in the
sieved self-raising flour, sugar, and salt along with the vanilla essence.
Pour into 2 greased and floured 8 inch (20cm) cake tins and bake in the
pre-heated oven for 30 minutes at 350 deg F (180 deg C) gas 4.

John Tovey
Miller Howe Hotel
Windermere
English Lakes

Biscuits

Points to watch when making biscuits.

Soft butter is a great help when making the doughs, and measure out your ingredients accurately.
Double-check the oven temperature. Domestic ovens can be as temperamental as the most fiendish prima donna - particularly when cooking biscuits. Of course, you look into the oven but you are only seeing the tops! What I find infuriating is when the tops are cooked, the bottoms (particularly those on trays placed on bottom shelves) are sometimes burnt. Just over halfway through cooking most biscuits, gently open the door and 'top and bottom' your trays.
A lot of people are then too hasty in the storing of their biscuits and pile them into containers whilst they are still hot. Always wait until the biscuits are stone cold and, seeing that you have taken time to prepare, shape and cook the biscuits, show a little care in the storing. Don't just slide the trayfuls into containers any old how. Stack biscuits neatly, then you will be able to one and all and not end up with a tin quarter full of broken bits.

Iced Coconut Biscuits

4 oz (100g) sieved plain flour
3 oz (75g) desiccated coconut
1 oz (25g) caster sugar
2 oz (50g) well-crushed cornflakes
4 oz (100g) butter

Mix all the dry ingredients in a bowl, pour on the melted butter and mix thoroughly together. Cover a baking sheet with greaseproof paper, and spoon out about 16 walnut-sized biscuits. Flatten each gently with a palette knife. Leave a little space round each one, but they do not spread much. Bake for 20 minutes at 350 deg F (180 deg C) gas 4. When cool, top with plain white icing (12oz (300g) icing sugar made up to the correct consistency with water).

Macaroons

1 oz (25g) sieved icing sugar
8 oz (225g) sieved caster sugar
6 oz (175g) ground almonds
3 egg whites
a drop of almond essence
about 36 - 40 whole almonds

Pre-heat the oven to 300 deg F (150 deg C) gas 2, and line the baking tray with rice paper.
Mix sugars and ground almonds together in a mixing bowl and make a well in the centre. Into this drop one egg white, and using a silver fork, work it into the sugar until you get a stiff smooth paste. Then gradually work in the other egg whites until the paste is soft and smooth. Flavour with almond essence.

Put the mixture into a piping bag with a star nozzle, and pipe
approximately 36 - 40 dainty sized biscuits onto the rice paper. Before
putting in the oven, dust with extra caster sugar and decorate each biscuit
with a whole almond. Bake for 30 minutes until firm and golden. Take out
and leave to cool, then trim off surplus rice paper and store in an
airtight container. These biscuits are deliciously nutty and chewy.

Banana Oatmeal Biscuits

This makes about 50 biscuits.

6 oz (175g) butter
6 oz (175g) caster sugar
1 egg, lightly beaten
6 oz (175g) plain flour
½ teaspoon bicarbonate of soda
1 teaspoon salt
½ teaspoon grated nutmeg
½ teaspoon powdered cinnamon
2 bananas, peeled and mashed
10 oz (275g) oatmeal
2 oz (50g) finely chopped peanuts

Pre-heat oven to 350 deg F (180 deg C) gas 4.
Cream the butter and sugar until light and fluffy, and then beat in the
egg. Sieve in the flour, bicarbonate of soda, salt and spices and fold in
the bananas, oatmeal and peanuts. Mix well.
Line a baking tray or trays with greaseproof paper. Using two teaspoons
(one for scooping and one for scraping the mixture off onto the trays)
spread heaped teaspoons of the mixture on the trays allowing about 2 inches
(5cm) between each biscuit as they will spread in the cooking.
Bake for 15 minutes and then transfer to a rack to cool. Remember to do
this as quickly as possible, otherwise the bottoms of the biscuits will
continue cooking with the heat of the tray and sometimes their bottoms get
slightly browner than one would like.

Miller Howe Fork Biscuits

10 oz (275g) sifted self-raising flour
4 oz (100g) caster sugar
8 oz (225g) fairly soft butter
grated rind of one large lemon

Place all four ingredients into a Kenwood bowl and use the K beater. Mix
slowly until the ingredients come together. At this stage the dough can
either be put in the deep freeze or kept in the fridge for up to a week.
When required, bring up to room temperature and form into small balls which
are flattened out onto a baking sheet using the back of a fork dipped in
cold water. Bake at 350 deg F (180 deg C) gas 4, for 10 minutes. As they
are cooling, sprinkle with vanilla sugar. When cold, store in air-tight
containers.

Vanilla Sugar

Every kitchen should have tucked away in a cupboard a small tin of this, as it has so many uses and does enhance so many biscuits etc. Simply find an empty tin or jar and place inside 2 or 3 vanilla pods and fill the tin up with caster sugar. To spinkle the sugar on, I use a large salt shaker (that you find in fish and chip shops) as the top comes off freely when you wish to fill up the container and when shaken the vanilla sugar comes out in force.

John Tovey
Miller Howe Hotel
Windermere
English Lakes

Marsala and Almond Cake

8 oz (225g) caster sugar
8 oz (225g) butter
4 eggs, lightly beaten
10 oz (275g) sieved self-raising flour
pinch of salt
4 oz (100g) ground almonds
6 tablesp Marsala, (if Marsala is not available use sweet sherry and
  change the name!)

This mixing will fill an 8 inch (20cm) square tin which has been lined with
a double layer of greaseproof paper. Set the oven to 350 deg F (170 deg C)
gas 3.
This cake is the better if you spend some time and care in really beating
the sugar and butter together until light and white and creamy, and then
slowly add the egg mixture a little at a time. Then all you do is gently
fold in the flour, salt, almonds and delicious Marsala. Bake at 350 deg
(170 deg C) gas 3 for 45 minutes and then turn off the oven, cover the cake
with foil and leave it in the oven for a further 45 minutes.
When cool, turn out the cake and prick deeply on top and base so that you
can spinkle liberally with further Marsala. I find this cake is very
popular and really loved by elderly people as it has a richness to it that
is easily digestible, and a lot of my older friends would rather I make
them one for Christmas as opposed to my very rich Christmas Cake (but
perhaps they don't like my Christmas Cake!)

Lemon Bread

6 oz (175g) butter
10 oz (275g) caster sugar
4 eggs, lightly beaten
5 oz (150g) self-raising flour
5 oz (150g) plain flour
4 oz (100g) chopped walnuts
rind and juice of 2 lemons

This recipe will bake 2 loaves, if you use 1 lb (450g) loaf tins. If you
have good non-stick tins, there is no need to prepare them, other wise I
suggest you line the tins well with good greaseproof paper.
Pre-heat the oven to 350 deg F (180C) gas 4.
Cream the butter and sugar together well until white and fluffy, and then
gradually beat in the lightly beaten eggs. Fold in both flours and chopped
nuts and then add the juice and rind of the lemons. Mix well.
Turn into prepared tins and bake for about 1 hour.

John Tovey
Miller Howe Hotel
Windermere
English Lakes

184

CHEERS! A guide to value-for-money enjoyment of festive drinking.

* Stock up on non-alcoholic options.
* Use wine as an aperitif (cheaper, more interesting and less alcoholic than spirits), for example:
    Kir - blackcurrant liqueur or fruit juice added to dry white wine or, for a Kir Royal, sparkling wine. Try fruit flavours too - peach is fashionable these days.
* Or a dessert wine, delicious with (unsalted) nuts.
* Or a spritzer - white wine and soda water.
* Do chill white wine - makes a magical difference to flavour and refreshment (an hour or two in the fridge).
* Warm red wine in a saucepan with added spices for a restorative punch.
* On average plan for six glasses per bottle.
* Look for wines bottled by the producer, ideally with "proprietaire - recoltant" on the label. Means "owner-grower", someone who cares about the quality of his wine.
* Pay a little more. The duty, shipping, handling and mark-up account for at least £2 on most bottles, so the wine value is minimal if you pay much less then £3. Ideally aim for about £4-£4.50 for decent characterful drinking.
* Talk to a local independent wine merchant: they are knowledgeable and care about the wines they sell.
* Waitrose, Sainsburys and M & S have good vintage selections: browse a little.
* Avoid non-vintage wines and 1984. 1987 is adequate: best are 1982, 1983, 1985 and 1986. Especially 1985.
* Avoid bottles standing up on high shelves or in windows. Wine needs careful storage and is damaged if the cork has dried out, or the bottle has been overheated or exposed to light for long periods.
* Buy Hugh Johnson's 'Pocket Book of Wine' (Mitchell Beazley). Not expensive for the amazingly good advice it gives. Also a good present.
* Real wine buffs should also read 'Websters Wine Guide' written by Oz Clarke and the 'Which? Wine Guide'.

Fun Ideas:

* Drink Beaujolais (can be slightly chilled) with fish and chips.
* Try Lebanon's miracle, Chateau Musar, produced in the Beirut battlefields. It's big, velvety, rich and excellent value compared to equivalent quality Bordeaux.
* "Vins de Pays" are mainly produced by co-operatives in France and many are excellent. If in doubt, choose red not white (cheaper reds are less variable in quality than cheap whites and less likely to be acidic).
* Buy a case (12 bottles) and get a discount. Over Christmas you'll drink enough to justify the saving. Take a few tasters home first and when you've found a winner, go for more, but quickly. The best bargains go fast in December.
* Try a dessert wine (especially Vouvray or Coteaux du Layon) with blue cheese; and with Christmas pud or mince pies.
* Look for Georges Duboeuf Beaujolais Nouveau, not one of the cheapest but usually one of the best and in a pretty painted bottle which looks fabulous

on the table. Also look for his other, "Flower Label" Beaujolais, for all
the same reasons.

Most of the above applies to French Wines. Some New World wines are
excellent but many are overpriced.

Cheers!

Rhiannon Chapman.

Glossary

Bain-marie:- a large pan of hot water, or 'bath' in which a smaller pan is placed for cooking contents or to keep foods warm. A double saucepan with water in the lower half. A baking pan containing water is often used as a bain-marie for cooking baked eggs, ramekins or mousses. Either on top of the stove or in the oven.

Ballotine:- a hot or cold dish, based on meat, poultry or fish in aspic.

Brunoise:- vegetables cut into very small dice aprroximately 2 mm or 1/16th inch square.

Chinois:- a conical sieve with a handle and a fine mesh.

Dariole Mould:- a small steep-sided, round mould, used for making puddings, sweet and savoury jellies and creams.

Demi-glace:- a rich brown sauce usually with added Madeira, sherry or similar.

Duxelle:- mixture of onions, shallots and mushrooms, chopped finely and cooked slowly in butter.

Fond:- another name for stock.

Frituese:- deep fryer.

Leaf gelatine:- highly refined gelatine produced in thin transparent, almost colourless sheets, approximately 3g (1/10 oz) each. Giving 7 - 9 sheets per 25g (1oz).

Mirepoix:- a mixture of finely diced vegetables and ham, which, when fried in butter is used as a base for brown sauces and stews.

Mousserons:- wild meadow mushrooms.

Panade:- a flour paste for thickening forcemeats. Also a type of soup made from bread, stock, milk (or water) and butter.

Salamander:- a type of oven in which the heat is directed down from the roof, used by professional cooks for glazing, browning and caramelising. The grill of a cooker can substitute for a salamander.

Tamari:- Japanese soya sauce.

Red Mullet baked with Braised Onion, Tomato and Thyme 55
Red Pepper Mousse 14
Redberry Soup 36
Rice Pudding, Hambleton's Toasted 144
Rillettes de Volaille et de Truite Fumee au Rifort 19
Rochers - Swiss Meringue Petits Fours 158
Rosemary and Courgette Soup 44
Rouille 74
Roulade, chilled, of Smoked Salmon and Sole Mousse 77
Roulade de Sole et Salmon an Mirepoix 62
Rum Truffles 159

Notes

Notes